Jhenah Telyndru has s. ...uu in beautifully weaving the complex, paradoxical nature of one of Wales' most beloved deities into a clear and inspirational work. Beautifully written with passion and devotion, this book is as fragrantly delicious and divine as the flowers that went into the magical making of Blodeuwedd. This is a delightful tome that is sure to be a go-to classic, filled with the inimitable sagacity of Telyndru, and her love for the Goddesses of this magical land.

Kristoffer Hughes, Head of the Anglesey Druid Order, author of *From the Cauldron Born: Exploring the magic of Welsh legend and Lore*

With dedicated scholarship and awen-inspired storytelling, Jhenah Telyndru has gifted us with a richly textured honouring of a complex Goddess. Not with oak, broom, and meadowsweet, but with historical source material, modern texts, and her own talon-sharp insight, Ms. Telyndru has crafted a revisioning of Blodeuwedd that elevates Her to a central role as a seasonal sovereignty Goddess rather than the uni-dimensional Goddess who was punished for the betrayal of Her husband.

It is time for Blodeuwedd to be given Her respectful and compassionate due. This book does that in spades, offering a deep exploration for all the intricate facets of Blodeuwedd's story while weaving in significant contextual information such as the shifting social mores of medieval Wales. Balancing a scholastic appreciation for the depth of this myth with the invitation to enter into relationship with the Goddess, Blodeuwedd: Welsh Goddess of Seasonal Sovereignty includes powerful workings that not only deepen a visceral, embodied understanding of the

Goddess, but open one to the experience of self that is complex, sovereign, and imbued with wisdom.

The world is well familiar with the light/dark aspects of the Greek Persephone in her dual role of Kore and Queen. How wonderful that there is finally a book that recognizes that same profound duality in Blodeuwedd – not as the Goddess who betrays but as the Sovereign seasonal queen around whom the sacred union with dark and light in turn hinges.

In the spirit of the true bard-priestess she is, Ms. Telyndru ends with a poetic homage to Blodeuwedd that uplifts as powerfully as the owl's wing. For the scholarship, for the poetry, for the brilliance, you want to read this book.

Tiffany Lazic, Psychotherapist and author of *The Great Work: Self-Knowledge and Healing Through the Wheel of the Year*

Pagan Portals - Blodeuwedd is an indispensable guide to this most beloved goddess from Welsh myth. Jhenah Telyndru makes excellent scholarly use of the sources, as well as drawing on her deep visionary experience to draw the spiritual wisdom from Blodeuwedd's tale, showing us the goddess in all her power as well as her beauty. This book is both owls and flowers, grounded in the traditional lore, and a beautiful, insightful read. Valuable for all those devoted to a Celtic spiritual path, as well as an excellent devotional to one of our most misunderstood Goddesses of Sovereignty.

Danu Forest, Traditional wisewoman and Celtic scholar, author of several books including *Wild Magic- Celtic Folk Traditions for the Solitary Practitioner*, and *Pagan Portals - Gwyn ap Nudd: Wild God of Faerie and Guardian of Annwfn*

Pagan Portals
Blodeuwedd

Welsh Goddess of Seasonal Sovereignty

Pagan Portals
Blodeuwedd

Welsh Goddess of Seasonal Sovereignty

Jhenah Telyndru

MOON
BOOKS

Winchester, UK
Washington, USA

JOHN HUNT PUBLISHING

First published by Moon Books, 2021
Moon Books is an imprint of John Hunt Publishing Ltd., No. 3 East Street, Alresford
Hampshire SO24 9EE, UK
office@jhpbooks.net
www.johnhuntpublishing.com
www.moon-books.net

For distributor details and how to order please visit the 'Ordering' section on our website.

Text copyright: Jhenah Telyndru 2020

ISBN: 978 1 78535 212 6
978 1 78535 922 4 (ebook)
Library of Congress Control Number: 2020939173

A CIP catalogue record for this book is available from the British Library.

Design: Stuart Davies

Printed and bound by CPI Group (UK) Ltd, Croydon, CR0 4YY
Printed in North America by CPI GPS partners

We operate a distinctive and ethical publishing philosophy in
all areas of our business, from our global network of authors to
production and worldwide distribution.

Contents

Acknowledgments

I am incredibly grateful to Dr. Jane Cartwright, with whom I had the honor to study at the University of Wales, Trinity St. David. She served as the academic advisor for my Master's dissertation, which focused on the role of Blodeuwedd as a Seasonal Sovereignty figure in the Fourth Branch of *Y Mabinogi*.

I am also deeply appreciative of the cultural insights and encouragement of my dear friend Kristoffer Hughes, Head of the Anglesey Druid Order and brilliant author and teacher. His service to the Gods of Wales is deeply inspirational: infused with love, informed by scholarship, and empowered with the Awen.

Endless thanks as well to artist Dan Goodfellow, who generously has permitted his inspired and inspiring painting of Blodeuwedd to grace the cover of this work.

I do not have enough words of thanks for the personal support and editorial skills of my beloved Sister in Avalon, Lori Feldmann. Cappys gonna Cap!

And finally, I am so honored to work with Trevor Greenfield, editor of Moon Books. Thank you so very much, Trevor, for all of your hard work, support, and understanding through every step of the publishing process.

Introduction

In the dawning light of a new beginning, she unfurls.
Petal-soft, her heady scent rises
 like the reborn sun
 and is carried by the breeze.
Crowned with golden strings of oak blossoms,
 an eagle shelters in her highest boughs.
Fortified in lattice-worked hedgerows,
 the sacred wren nests
 beneath the flowers of riotous yellow broom,
 spreading laughter
 across the brightening landscape.
Cresting like sea foam
 from beyond the ninth wave,
 the white caps of meadowsweet break like a rising tide
 as the sun reaches his apex above.
Now a bride's bouquet...
Now a maiden's funerary offering...
The Queen of the Meadow follows
 the lengthening shadows
 to the very edges of her sovereign realm.

There, by riverbank and holey-stone,
 the seven-tined stag awaits her -
 his milk-white body presaging
 the rising of the moon.
The sun slips below the horizon
 to seek his rest in the islands of the west.
Side by side, they ford the river
 her arms outstretched
 her voice raised in song.
All as the Silver Wheel weaves a diamond tapestry

in the deep night sky.
Her eyes grow wide as apples
Her long white fingers form
a fringe of feathers.
Her feet become talons,
become vise grips,
become weapons.
Her body shifts, like a ghost in the night.
Her wings unfurl in the growing
dark of a new day.

Who is Blodeuwedd?

A Goddess? A nature spirit? A magical conjuration? An embodiment of the land?

Until recent years, the story of Blodeuwedd was rarely known outside of Wales itself, and those familiar with her tale did not generally hold her in very high regard. For non-Welsh speakers, her very name is challenging; hard to spell, difficult to pronounce - and she has two of them! First, she is called *Blodeuedd* (bluh-DYE-eth), "Flowers", after the components from which she is created. Later, she is renamed *Blodeuwedd* (bluh-DYE-weyth), which means "Flower Face or Flower Aspect", in acknowledgment of her owl form. *(Please note: for simplicity's sake, except for times when she is being specifically being discussed in her aspect of the Flower Bride, this book refers to her as Blodeuwedd throughout.)*

No matter what she may once have been, Blodeuwedd's literary legacy is that of a magical woman conjured out of flowers for the sole purpose of becoming the wife of Lleu, a prince who was prohibited from marrying a human woman. She eventually came to betray her husband, falling in love with a neighboring lord and conspiring to kill Lleu in order to be with her lover. In the end, she is punished by her creator by being turned into an owl - that most hated of birds - cursed to never again dwell in the light of day.

Overwhelmingly, Blodeuwedd is perceived in a negative light. At best, her shortcomings can be blamed on her naivety; after all, what could be expected of this weak and simple creature created out of flowers, formed as a fully-grown woman with no life experience, having had no mother to raise her or guide her on her role as wife? At worst, however, she is the embodiment of the evils of women who give into their wanton sexual desires, who plot against the men in their lives, and who defy the social contract by seeking to circumvent the roles and expectations placed upon them by the over-culture.

In medieval Wales, Blodeuwedd's story likely served as a cautionary tale intended to dissuade women, especially, from trying to break free from the confines placed upon them by society. Her punishment demonstrates that nothing good can come from seeking to change the circumstances of one's life beyond what is considered proper... and what is proper is for women to be faithful to their husbands, to fulfill their wifely duties, and to never give in to the lustful failings of the flesh.

To the modern reader, Blodeuwedd's story can be challenging in many respects, and reactions to her are likewise quite varied. Some who read her tale with modern eyes see a woman who acted against her apparently loving husband with unwarranted cruelty; adultery is one thing, but why didn't she just leave Lleu, instead of conspiring to kill him? Others see Blodeuwedd as an early paragon of feminism, a heroine who fought to escape the limitations of what she was expected to be, and risked everything she had in order to live a life of her own choosing.

Whether cast as feckless naif, manipulative vixen, or driven freedom fighter, the maiden who begins her tale as a Flower Bride ends it in the form of an owl. Perhaps this was, as it appears on the surface, an act of punishment intended to dissuade others from making similar choices. Perhaps her owl form is an unconscious symbol of the vilification of women's power by the patriarchy - which, having tried and failed to control her, was forced instead to banish her into the darkness of the collective Shadow. Perhaps her transformation was but a revelation of her truest form. Perhaps, through her choices, she obtained the wisdom of the owl and the freedom of her wings.

Blodeuwedd's story is a complex weaving of several strands of tradition. Obtaining as clear an understanding as possible of her many facets will allow us to develop the foundation necessary to come into deep relationship with her as a deity.

To get a sense of who she may once have been, we must first examine the meaning of her tale from the perspective of those who passed the story on and eventually came to write it down. We can then use these insights to engage in a kind of mythic archaeology in order to identify the symbols and folkloric motifs which have become embedded in Blodeuwedd's tale over time.

Once unearthed from the narrative, we can use these pieces of information to embark upon a journey that allows us to reclaim Blodeuwedd - not only as the Goddess she may have once been, but as a deity who has risen once again into our collective consciousness for a reason. I believe that part of this reason is that she holds lessons which can assist us as individuals to grow into our true and authentic selves, and because she is a powerful and necessary ally for the challenges that face our world in the here and now.

Blodeuwedd is so much more than a uni-dimensional figure in a cautionary tale intended to keep women in their place. Reclaiming her as a fully-realized deity with agency and power requires that we understand the medieval context of her tale, retrace the details of her obscured divinity, and restore her role as a seasonal Sovereignty figure.

And so, let us begin.

Chapter 1

Legend and Lore

The story of Blodeuwedd is primarily known to us from the Fourth Branch of *Y Mabinogi,* a medieval Welsh story cycle. Although current scholarship dates the extant manuscripts containing the Four Branches to the 12th century, aspects of these tales are thought to be of much older origin, believed to have been transmitted from generation to generation through oral tradition.

The Fourth Branch, also known by the title "Math ap Mathonwy", can be broken down into three distinct but interrelated story arcs, and although Blodeuwedd only appears in the last third of the tale, it is important to read the Branch in its entirety to understand the events leading up to her creation.

A Retelling of the Fourth Branch

The song of Blodeuwedd is a shimmering verse in a long and branching tale. It is a bend in a sacred river fed by a confluence of many streams. To speak only of the river is to discount its journey through many lands - lands which both shaped, and were shaped by, its waters. Each tributary brings its story along with it, each becoming a chapter in the history of the whole river - each contributing its voice to the song.

To begin, then, we must sing first of the court of Math, brother of Great Dôn and king of Gwynedd in the north of Wales. A powerful magician, he possessed several peculiarities: first, that no word could be spoken anywhere that the wind would not take up and whisper into his ear, and second that he could not live unless his feet rested in the lap of a virgin. It is because of this necessity that Math could not circuit his lands in the way of Welsh lords, and so Gwydion and Gilfaethwy, the sons of his sister, did so in his stead.

Now it came to pass that Gilfaethwy had fallen madly in love with Goewin, his uncle's footholder, and he fell sick with his longing for her. When he confessed his situation to Gwydion - who, like their uncle, was a great enchanter - his brother promised he would find a way to remedy the situation.

It is here that our song turns dark. Knowing that Math could only be parted from his footholder when called to lead his warriors into battle, Gwydion set out to instigate a war with the kingdom of Dyfed in the south. The ruler of Dyfed was Pryderi, son of Rhiannon and Pwyll, and he possessed fantastic pigs gifted to him by Arawn, king of the Otherworldly realm of Annwn. Pryderi was oath-bound not to gift any of these pigs until they had doubled in number, but clever-tongued Gwydion convinced him that trading was different from giving - and oh, what wonders had Gwydion to trade with him!

For, in secret, the magician had gathered some toadstools and used them to conjure horses and hounds, saddles and shields - the finest ever seen. The dazzled Pryderi was eager to trade - and the cunning Gwydion was eager to leave, for the magic of his illusion would stand only for one day. Once Pryderi realized he had traded his Otherworldly pigs for an enclosure full of mushrooms, he mustered his forces against Gwynedd.

In response to Dyfed's attack, Math had no choice but to lead his army into battle - leaving Goewin behind at his court, Caer Dathyl. Thus alone, Gilfaethwy raped her in Math's own bed - all because Gwydion lit the flames of war so his brother could sate his lust. And so, we sing of a betrayal of trust between woman and man, between nephew and uncle, between North Wales and South, and between nobles and those who die for their causes.

In the midst of the clash, Pryderi calls upon Gwydion to meet him on the field of honor, warrior to warrior, so that no one else should die because of the wrong Gwydion had done to him. The son of Dôn agreed to meet Pryderi in combat, but no matter how valiantly he fought, the son of Rhiannon fell before Gwydion's sword and enchantments. Thus defeated, the South retreated, and the war was ended.

Calling for Goewin upon returning to his court, Math learns of her rape and the betrayal of his nephews. To make amends for the great wrong done to her, Math marries Goewin and makes her his queen, giving her authority over his lands. Though they sought to avoid him, Gwydion and Gilfaethwy were eventually forced to stand before their uncle to answer for their crimes.

Let us sing now of Math's magic and the three years he punished his nephews, transforming them into pairs of animals compelled to obey the urgings of their nature. Stag and hind, boar and sow, he-wolf and she-wolf they became... losing their form, their identity, their very names. Each year, in turn, one bore a son to the other - first Gilfaethwy, then Gwydion, then Gilfaethwy once more. Each year these offspring returned to Math's court, where they were struck with his wand and became human children. The names Math gave them recalled their animal origins - Little Deer Man, Little Pig Man, Little Wolf Man - and the three were kept in bardic memory with the following triad:

Three sons of Gilfaethwy the False -
Three warriors true: Bleidwn, Hydwn and Hychdwn the Tall

After three years, with their punishments over, Math's nephews are restored to their humanity and to their uncle's friendship. Although we hear no more of Gilfaethwy, Gwydion takes his place at Math's court once again.

And so, our song shifts, and a new tune begins, for in response to Math's need to find a new footholder, Gwydion suggests his sister Arianrhod. Daughter of Dôn, niece of Math, lady of her own court on an island bearing her name off the seacoast of Wales - she comes to Caer Dathyl when Math calls her.

"Are you a virgin?" Math asks.

"I do not know otherwise," she answers.

"We shall see," he replies, bending his magic wand and instructing her to step over it.

Raising her skirts, parting her knees, lifting one foot then the other, Arianrhod steps over the wand - and from her falls a yellow-haired infant boy. The baby cries out, and Arianrhod runs from the court, dropping a small thing from her as she goes. This small thing is taken up by Gwydion, who wraps it in brocade silk, and places it in a wooden chest by his bed. Math, in the meantime, has named the baby Dylan ("Great Tide") and baptizes him in the way of the time. Once receiving his name, Dylan makes his way to the sea and takes its nature immediately upon entering the waters. He is remembered as Dylan ail Tôn - Dylan of the Waves - for no wave was known to break beneath him. He was later accidentally killed by an unfortunate blow struck by his uncle Gofannon.

Sometime after Dylan disappeared into the sea, Gwydion hears a sound from the chest in his chamber. Opening it, he sees the arms of a baby boy reaching for him, emerging from the brocade that swaddled him. Finding a wet nurse and then rearing the child at court, Gwydion came to love the boy above all others. The child was strong and grew quickly, and after only four years had passed, he easily appeared to be more than twice his age in size and intellect.

Eventually, Gwydion brings the child with him to visit his sister's court at Caer Arianrhod, where she greets Gwydion warmly and enquires after the boy's identity. She becomes angry when he tells her that he is her own son, and asks why he's kept this reminder of her shame for so long. Gwydion argues that he has done the right thing in fostering so fine a boy, and tells her that he does not yet have a name.

Arianrhod then places a *tynged*, or destiny, upon the boy saying, "He will have no name save one I give to him!"

"You are a wicked woman," Gwydion replies, "because you are angry that you are no longer called a maiden. But I promise you, he will get a name!"

Storming off with the boy, the two spend the night at Caer Dathyl. Rising early the next morning, Gwydion takes the child with him for a walk along the seashore. Using the seaweed he gathered together from along the strand, Gwydion conjures a ship with a sail, and a hold full of the finest Cordovan leather in fantastic colors never before seen. Using his magics to disguise their appearance, he and the boy set sail for the harbor of Caer Arianrhod, peddling their services as a master shoemaker and his apprentice. Word of their beautiful creations came to Arianrhod, who sends them her measurements so they might craft a pair of shoes for her. Gwydion creates several pairs of ill fitting, yet beautiful shoes for Arianrhod. Wondering at how such a skilled craftsman could make such incredible shoes, yet not be able to size them correctly, Arianrhod visits his ship in person so that he can take measurements directly from her feet.

As the disguised Gwydion does so, a tiny wren lands on the deck of the ship. Picking up a stone, the young apprentice casts it at the bird, striking its leg between the tendon and the bone. Impressed with his skill, Arianrhod exclaims, "The fair one has a skillful hand!" and with that, the enchantment fell away, revealing Gwydion and the boy for who they were. "Lady," Gwydion proclaims, "you have just named your son!" And from that day he was called Lleu Llaw Gyffes, the phrase Arianrhod uttered in her amazement.

Angry at her brother's trickery, Arianrhod lays a new destiny upon the boy, forbidding him to bear arms unless she herself armed him. Gwydion and Lleu depart, taking up residence at Dinas Dinlle. There the boy continued to grow, becoming skilled in horsemanship but restless in his desire to train in arms. One day, promising Lleu a solution, the pair return to Caer Arianrhod, disguised as traveling bards, Arianrhod welcomes them to her court with a feast. Gwydion, who was an excellent storyteller, entertained the assembly late into the night.

Rising early from the guest chamber where he and Lleu slept, Gwydion called upon his magic once more. As the dawn broke, a battle alarm rang out as a great fleet of invading ships sailed into view on the horizon. In a frenzy, the island began preparing for its defense, and in the midst of the panic, Arianrhod and her women suited up and armed the two bards. As she unwittingly handed her now-armored son a sword, the fleet disappeared and the men's disguises fell away, revealing Gwydion and Lleu to an outraged Arianrhod.

Angry at Gwydion's deceit and for terrorizing her people, Arianrhod lays one last destiny upon her son: that he was forbidden to marry a woman of the race of the Earth. Declaring her a wicked woman once more, the pair return to Math's court, where Gwydion consults with his uncle on what to do next. By this time, Lleu had grown into a strong and handsome youth, ready to step fully into his manhood.

And so, our song shifts into its third and final verse, as the two magicians combine their wit and their spellcraft to aid Lleu Llaw Gyffes. Gathering together the flowers of oak, broom, and meadowsweet, Gwydion and Math conjure forth a woman to be Lleu's bride. They baptized her in the manner of the day and named her Blodeuedd, which means "flowers". The wedding feast was held that very night. Now possessing a name, arms, and a wife, Math gifts Lleu lands of his own, the cantref of Dinoding, to rule over from its seat at Mur Castell.

The newlyweds lived there happily for a time, and one day Lleu set out to visit Math at Caer Dathyl, leaving the holding in the care of Blodeuedd. Later that same day, Gronw Pebyr, lord of the neighboring kingdom of Penllyn, was engaged in a stag hunt that crossed into Lleu's land. It was almost sunset when Gronw finally brought down the stag, and he dressed it on the banks of the River Cynfael. Hearing that the neighboring lord and his hunting party had tarried late on her lands, Blodeuedd extended the hospitality of her hall to them, as was the custom.

At the feast, Blodeuedd and Gronw found themselves infused with love for each other, and spent the night in each other's arms. The next morning, Gronw sought to take his leave, but Blodeuedd asked him to remain with her another day, and they spent a second night in lovemaking. The next day, Gronw again moved to depart, but Blodeuedd asked him to stay with her once more, and they spent a third night together. When again morning came, the couple agreed that he should leave that day, but before he did so, the two conspired to find a way they could remain together forever.

Not long after Gronw and his party departed, Lleu returned home. That night in their bed, Lleu sensed a difference in his wife, and asked what troubled her. She replied, "While you were gone, I came to worry about what might happen should you be killed and not return home to me."

Touched by her apparent concern, Lleu responded, "Oh, you needn't worry about that; it is not easy for me to be killed."

"What do you mean?" she inquired.

"Well, I cannot be killed indoors nor outdoors, nor on foot or on horseback. And the only weapon that could harm me is one that is forged over a year and a day during prayers on Sundays."

"That sounds like something that could never happen," she replied.

"That is assured," he responded. "So, you need not fear for me. The only way it could happen is if I were to stand beneath a roof with no walls, with one foot on the edge of a tub and the other on the back of a beast. It is only then that the year-long forged weapon could kill me."

"That is a relief," Blodeuedd agreed. And the next day, she sent word to Gronw with instructions on how to forge the needed weapon.

After a year and a day had passed, Blodeuedd asked Lleu to

meet her on the banks of the River Cynfael. There, she had set up a bath for him under a thatched roof with no walls. Delighted by this gift, Lleu entered the warmth of the tub, and when he had finished bathing, Blodeuedd said, "Remember when you assured me that you couldn't be killed except under special circumstances? I just want to be sure that this is indeed the case, and that you are safe."

Bringing a goat buck to stand beside the tub, she asked Lleu to stand with one foot on the edge of the vessel and the other on the back of the animal. Happy to reassure her, Lleu did as she asked. As soon as he was in position - neither indoors nor out, neither on foot nor on horseback - Gronw rose up from his nearby hiding place, and let loose the spear he had worked on for a year of Sundays. The weapon hit its mark, and with a scream, Lleu transformed into an eagle and flew away.

With Lleu gone, Blodeuedd and Gronw made for Mur Castell, and began to rule over the merged lands of Dinoding and Penllyn.

It was not long before Gwydion got word of what had transpired, and set out to find his beloved nephew. Wandering all of Wales in search of Lleu, he came to spend the night in Arfon where he heard of a strange occurrence. Each morning, when a swineherd opened the gate of his pen, one of his sows would disappear into the countryside; no-one knew where she went, but she would return every evening, fat and satiated. The next morning, Gwydion rose early and followed the sow, who rushed upstream along a brook, only stopping beneath a tree where she started to eat. When Gwydion caught up with her, he looked up to see a wounded eagle roosted on the highest branches of an enormous oak tree. When the eagle flapped its wings, pieces of rotting flesh and maggots fell from its body to the ground below, which was eagerly devoured by the sow.

Certain that this eagle was his missing nephew, Gwydion tapped the oak three times with his wand as he recited the following *englynion*, or poetic verses:

Oak that grows between the two banks;
Darkened is the sky and hill!
Shall I not tell him by his wounds,
That this is Lleu?

Oak that grows in upland ground,
Is it not wetted by the rain? Has it not been drenched
By nine score tempests?
It bears in its branches Lleu Llaw Gyffes!

Oak that grows beneath the steep;
Stately and majestic is its aspect!
Shall I not speak it?
That Lleu will come to my lap?
(From "Math ap Mathonwy", Lady Charlotte Guest, trans.)

After each verse, the eagle descended into lower branches of the tree until, after the last line was spoken, it came to rest on Gwydion's lap. The magician touched the eagle with his wand, and it transformed back into the weak and gravely wounded Lleu. Gwydion brought his nephew to Caer Dathyl where the best physicians and healers in the land came to care for Lleu. It wasn't until the end of the year that his health was finally restored. Ready now to redress the wrongs done to him, and wanting to reclaim his lands, Lleu told Math his intention, and they gathered the forces of Gwynedd.

Gwydion marched ahead of the war band and made his way to Mur Castell to face Blodeuedd for her part in the betrayal of Lleu. Terrified, Blodeuedd gathered her women and fled, seeking the protection of a court nestled in the mountains, on the other side of the River Cynfael. With Gwydion in pursuit, the frightened women ran as quickly as they could, glancing behind them after every few steps to determine how close their pursuer was becoming. As the darkness grew, so did their panic, and because they were so concerned with what was happening behind them, the women did not pay attention to what was happening in front of them - and one by one, all but Blodeuedd fell into a lake and drowned. In their memory, the lake is now called Llyn Morwynion, the Lake of the Maidens.

Alone now and exhausted, Blodeuedd was finally overtaken by Gwydion. Standing over her, he declared his judgement, "I will punish you for your shaming of Lleu Llaw Gyffes, but I will not destroy you. Instead, I will transform you into an owl for all time. You will never be able to show your face again in the light of day, for you will be hated by all other birds and they will attack you on sight. And you will keep your name, forever to be called Blodeuwedd." With that, he touched her with his magic wand, turning her into an owl. To this day in Wales *blodeuwedd*, which means "Flower Face", is a word for owl.

At the same time, Gronw retreated to Penllyn and sent Lleu an offer of land and gold as recompense for the matter between them. Lleu replied that he would only be satisfied by the lord of Penllyn meeting him on the banks of the River Cynfael. There, each of them would stand where the other had stood, and Lleu would cast his spear at Gronw.

Upon receiving this message, Gronw turned to his men, and asked if any of them would stand in his place, which was the custom of the time. No-one came forward to protect their lord, and Gronw's retinue became known as one of the Three Disloyal War Bands of the Island of the Mighty.

Having no choice but to take the blow for himself, Gronw met Lleu on the river bank, and asked, "Since this situation was instigated by a woman, may I at least hold this slab of stone between us when you cast your spear?"

"Although it is more consideration than you granted me, I will allow it," Lleu responded.

The two men got into position - Lleu with his spear, and Gronw with his stone shield. Lleu hurled his weapon at Gronw so powerfully that it pierced the stone and Gronw's heart both, breaking his back and killing him on the spot. To this day, on the banks of the River Cynfael can be found an upright of stone, about chest-high on a man, with a hole through the center of it, and it is called Llech Ronw - Gronw's Stone. With that, Lleu was avenged, and took back his land.

Thus, ends our song.

Thus, ends this Branch of Y Mabinogi.

Other Sources

While the Fourth Branch of Y Mabinogi contains the most complete extant version of Blodeuwedd's story, she and her tale are referenced in other medieval Welsh writings as well. Several poems from the 14th century manuscript Llyfr Taliesin (The Book of Taliesin) - which contains poems believed to date back as far as the 6th century CE - appear to allude to Blodeuwedd. One of them, "Cad Goddeu" ("Battle of the Trees"), does not directly name Blodeuwedd, but a section of the poem seems to be an account of her creation by Math and Gwydion. We will discuss this poem further in Chapter 5.

Another poem from Llyfr Taliesin, "Cadair Ceridwen" ("The Chair of Ceridwen"), includes these lines:

Celfyddaf gwr a gigleu
Gwydion ap Don dygnferthau
A hudwys gwraig a Elodeu

The most skilful man ever heard of
(Was) Gwydion ap Don, a hard toiler,
Who made by enchantment, a woman from flowers.

An interesting verse, called "The Deceiving of Huan" is found in

Peniarth MS 112 880-881, dating to sometime before 1619. Written several centuries after the medieval redaction of *Y Mabinogi*, it is quite short, and appears to be either a variant or later evolution of the tale recounted in the Fourth Branch.

Gwraig Huan ap Gwydion, a vu un o ladd ei gwr, ag a ddyfod ei fyned ef i hely oddi gartref, ai dad ef Gwdion brenhin Gwynedd y gerddis bob tir yw amofyn, ac or diwedd y gwnaeth ef Gaergwdion (sef: via laactua) sy yn yr awyr yw geissio: ag yn y nef y cafas ei chwedyl , lle yr oedd ei enaid: am hynny y troes y wraig iefanc yn ederyn, a ffo rhag ei thad yn y gyfraith, ag a elwir er hynny hyd heddiw Twyll huan.

The wife of Huan ap Gwydion was a party to the killing of her husband, and she said that he had gone to hunt away from home. And his father, Gwydion, the King of Gwynedd, traversed all countries in search of him, and at last made Caer Gwydion, that is the *via lactea*, which is in the sky, to seek him. And he found him in heaven, where was his soul. And for that he turned the young wife into a bird and she fled from her father-in-law, and is called to this day Twyll Huan (Huan's Deceiving*).*

It's fairly clear that this verse refers to the story of Blodeuwedd and Lleu, although she is not directly mentioned, and Lleu's name is given as Huan, which means "sun". We will discuss the meaning of Lleu's name in more detail later on in this work, but one theory is that it comes from the Proto-Indo-European word *leuk-*, meaning "light"; this etymology has been questioned by some modern linguists, but this verse gives some support to the idea of Lleu having some solar associations, as we shall see.

It is notable that "The Deceiving of Huan" directly states something that is only hinted at in the Fourth Branch: Gwydion appears to have traditionally been considered the father of Lleu.

Subtextual clues exist in the original Welsh of the Fourth Branch, where, in speaking with Gwydion about her yet-unnamed son, Arianrhod refers to the child as "your son/boy" (she uses the word *mab*, which means both son and boy), although this could may also be a reference to Gwydion's role as a surrogate mother and foster father to the boy. That said, this phrasing, especially in the context of the underlying shame that Arianrhod expresses when Gwydion brings the child before her, may support the theory of an incestuous origin for Lleu - a somewhat common occurrence in divine families throughout world mythology.

Finally, Gwydion's association with the *Via Lactea*, the Milky Way, in "The Deceiving of Huan" is significant not only because this presents an onomastic explanation for the existence of the Milky Way, but it also names this celestial body *Caer Gwydion* (Gwydion's Fortress) in much the same way as the constellation *Cassiopeia* is known in Wales as *Llys Dôn* (The Court of Dôn) after Gwydion's mother, and the *Corona Borealis* (Northern Crown) is called *Caer Arianrhod,* for his sister. The name Arianrhod, which means "Silver Wheel" may also refer to the roundness of the moon or the turning of her cycles. Although certainly evocative, it is unknown if these celestial associations with members of the House of Dôn - and particularly with Lleu/Huan, Arianrhod, and Gwydion as sun, moon, and stars - are reflective of earlier tradition or if they are contemporary to the author of this verse.

While modern scholars generally agree that Gwydion is the father of Lleu based on the subtext in the Fourth Branch, as mentioned above, there is also some evidence that Math himself may be his father, and indeed, father of Blodeuwedd as well. A late medieval Welsh genealogical tract called *Bonedd yr Arwyr* lists the children of Math ap Mathonwy as Lleu Llaw Gyffes, Dylan Eil Ton, and Blodeuwedd; Arianrhod, daughter of Dôn, is listed as their mother. As Dôn is Math's sister, this would mean that Arianrhod is Math's niece; further incest is suggested with Lleu and Blodeuwedd presented as being brother and sister.

However, since it was Arianrhod's final *tynged* on Lleu which led to the creation of Blodeuwedd by Math and Gwydion, she could potentially be considered Blodeuwedd's mother, by two fathers. Further, as Dylan and Lleu were born as a result of Arianrhod stepping over Math's wand during his chastity test - whether this act is read as a metaphor for intercourse or if the literal magic of his wand catalyzed the birth of these brothers - it makes sense for Math to have been considered their father as well.

A poem called "Achau y dylluan" ("The Pedigree of the Owl") - attributed, with some uncertainty, to the famous medieval Welsh poet Dafydd ap Gwilym - sees the poet asking questions of an owl about her name and history. She replies with the story familiar to us from the Fourth Branch, but adds a piece of information: that her father is the son of Meirchion, lord of Môn.

Bonedd gwellwedd i'm gelwynt;
Blodeuwedd wrlh gyfedd gynt:
Merch i arglwydd, ail Meirchion,
Wyf fi, myn Dewi! O Fon.

Celtic scholar John Rhys believes that Môn, or Anglesey, was used as a literary device to represent the Islands of the Otherworld in early Welsh vernacular tales and poetry. This couplet, therefore, may be reinforcing Blodeuwedd's connection to the Otherworld. In support of this, another poem, by Anthony Powell, who died in the early 17th century, describes Blodeuwedd as the daughter of Meirchion Lwyd (Grey Meirchion). It also states that she was overtaken by Gwydion near Craig y Ddinas in the Neath valley, where she is buried. (Rhys, 439).

Crug ael, carn gadarn a godwyd yn fryn,
Yn hen fraenwaith bochlwyd;
Main a'i llud man y lladdwyd,

Merrh hoewen loer Meirchson lwyd

Heaped on a brow, a mighty cairn built like a hill,
Like ancient work rough with age, grey-cheeked;
Stones that confine her where she was slain,
Grey Meirchion's daughter quick and bright as the moon.

Concerning Lleu

To fully understand Blodeuwedd's significance and nature, it is essential to also explore the mythological pedigree and lineage of her intended mate. Lleu is an important figure in Welsh mythos, a fact which is underscored by his connections to powerful divinities from other Celtic lands. Both he and the Irish God Lugh/Lug are cognates of the continental Celtic deity Lugus, who is known to us primarily through Gallo-Roman iconography and a few inscriptions which date back to the first century CE. However, an abundance of Lugus-derived toponyms and tribal names in Celtic areas of Europe and Britain, suggests he is a much older divinity. As they appear in much later literary records, Lugh and Lleu are likely culturally specific evolutions of Lugus, who is considered a pan-Celtic god.

Although the meaning of their names is unclear and has been a point of debate, there are several etymological possibilities. Some sources believe that Lleu shares the same etymological root as the words *golau* ("light, fair, bright") and *lleuad* ("moon") in Modern Welsh. Early linguists thought the name derives from the Proto-Indo-European *leuk-* which means "to shine" or "flashing light", a belief which supports the common notion that these were solar deities, or potentially related to other Indo-European gods of thunder. However, linguists have since determined that Proto-Indo-European *-k-* did not evolve into the Proto-Celtic *-g-*, making this etymology improbable. (Schrijver, 348). Currently, linguists believe the name more likely derives from Proto-Indo-European root words *leuǵ-* "to break", *leug-*

"black", or *leugʰ- "to swear an oath". The latter connection has caused many scholars to believe that Lugus was a god of oaths and contracts. (Wood, 30)

Some translations of the Fourth Branch give Lleu's name as Llew, which means "lion". Scholars believe this to be related to variations in early Welsh spelling, or to have been a transcription error which continued to be replicated. Lleu is likely the originally intended name because it matches the rhyming scheme of the Englynion Gwydion - the three verses Gwydion sang to coax the eagle-form of Lleu out of the oak tree - which is considered the oldest segment of the Four Branches. (Koch, 1166)

After the Roman conquest of Gaul, Celtic divinities were commonly syncretized with Roman gods with whom they shared similarities, a process called *interpretatio Romana*. This functioned, in part, to permit indigenous worship to continue side by side with the Imperial cultus. In his commentaries on the Gallic Wars, Julius Caesar writes of the Gauls:

"Of all the gods they most worship Mercury. He has the largest number of images, and they regard him as the inventor of all the arts, as their guide on the roads and in travel, and as chiefly influential in making money and in trade." (Caes. Gal. 6.17)

Scholars believe that Caesar is here referring to Lugus, who is commonly syncretized with Mercury in Gallo-Roman iconography and inscriptions. He is depicted with familiar symbols of the youthful Roman god, including the caduceus and winged sandals - indicating his connection to the healing arts, his status as a psychopomp who bridges the worlds, and his role as patron of travelers - as well as bags of coins, roosters, and a spear. Significantly, he was also a god of contracts, supporting his connection with Lugus as a god of oaths. When Lugus is depicted in a more Celtic fashion, he is bearded and sometimes tricephalic, indicating he may have been a triple deity. Several extant inscriptions refer to him as Lugoues, a plural form of his name, and he seems to have had a triple function: that of magician, warrior, and craftsman. Indeed, there is a famous dedication to Lugoues in Spain which was sponsored by a shoemaker's guild. (Koch, 1203)

Gallo-Roman iconography often pairs Mercury with the Celtic Goddess Rosmerta, whose name potentially means "Great Provider." Her attributes are the cornucopia, a Roman libation cup called a *patera,* and a large vessel, sometimes interpreted as a bucket or casket of mead. Rosmerta is also sometimes shown with the caduceus and winged sandals of Mercury, both when depicted alongside him and when alone, suggesting that she was a healing divinity in her own right. (Koch, 1542) Her association with the abundance of the land, as well as her potential connection to mead - which has ritual associations with the granting of kingship - may indicate her status as a Goddess of Sovereignty. That she often appears alongside a spear-bearing deity who is the inventor of all crafts and has the ability to travel between the worlds, is of particular interest to us as we seek to understand the meaning that underscores the narrative of the Fourth Branch.

Looking now at Insular Celtic tradition, Lleu holds many resonances with Lugh of Ireland, who is directly identified as a divinity in early literature. Lugh is a king of the Tuatha Dé Danann, while Lleu is a descendant of the House of Dôn, and eventually becomes king of Gwynedd. In the *Baile in Scáil* (*The Phantom's Frenzy*), Lugh appears in a vision to the warrior Conn, accompanied by a female figure identified as the Sovereignty of Ireland. Wearing a golden crown and bearing a golden cup, she asks Lugh to whom the cup should be given, and he lists Conn and all of the kings of Ireland who will come after him. Having a connection to Goddesses of Sovereignty seems to be an attribute that Lleu, Lugh, and Lugus/Mercury hold in common. They both bear similar epithets: compare Lleu Llaw Gyffes (Lleu of the Skillful Hand) with Lugh Lámhfhada (Lugh of the Long Arm) and Lugh Samildanach (Lugh of Many Skills). They are both associated with sling stones and spears. Both are craftsmen, with Lugh particularly praised in the *Cath Maige Tuired* (*The Second Battle of Moytura*) as being a builder, a smith, a champion, a harper, a warrior, a poet and a historian, a sorcerer, a physician, a cupbearer, and a brazier.

Lleu's facility with crafts are not as well-developed as those of Lugh in the extant literature, but his association with shoemakers is clear in the Fourth Branch, as well as in a Triad which names him as one of the Three Golden Shoemakers of the Island of Britain which, notably, further connects him to Lugus, who was patron of shoemakers, as mentioned above. We see Lleu disguised as a bard along with Gwydion on one of their visits to Caer Arianrhod, and there are references to his magical skills elsewhere in Welsh tradition. In *Cad Goddeu* (*The Battle of the Trees*), for example, Lleu assists Gwydion in raising an army of enchanted trees to battle Arawn, King of Annwn.

Aside from his ability with a spear, we see little of Lleu's battle prowess in the narrative of the Fourth Branch, although several early Welsh sources depict Lleu as a great warrior. A variant of Triad 20 from *Trioedd Ynys Prydein* names Lleu as one of the Three Red Ravagers of the Island of Britain, and in *Englynion y Beddau* (*The Stanzas of the Graves*) Lleu is remembered as "a man who spared no one".

In the same way the Gaulish god Lugus has given his name to several cities in Europe - including Leon in France, and Leiden in Germany (which are all believed to derive from the name *Lugudunum*, meaning Fort of Lugus) - several landscape areas mentioned in the Fourth Branch bear Lleu's name to this day. These include Dinas Dinlle - the Iron Age fort on the Welsh coast overlooking the sea where Caer Arianrhod is believed to have been - and Dyffryn Nantlle (literally, "The Valley of Lleu's

Stream"), the setting for some events in the Fourth Branch.

Taken altogether, it is clear from even this brief overview that Lleu is somewhat more than the human hero he is presented as being in the Fourth Branch. Not only is he a figure with an ancient pedigree and a divine heritage, but the snippets of Welsh lore concerning him that remain outside of the Fourth Branch suggests that he once featured in a much wider corpus of myth that has been lost to us. If Lleu, like many of the main characters in *Y Mabinogi*, was once divine, how does this help to inform our understanding of Blodeuwedd's true nature?

Let us explore further.

Chapter 2

Culture and Context

Because the Celtic Britons, like other Celtic peoples, opted to transmit their sacred stories solely through the vehicle of oral tradition, we have a very incomplete understanding of their Gods, their beliefs, and their religious practices. Most of what we do know comes to us from the archaeological record, the sometimes-biased accounts of contemporary cultures like the ancient Greeks and Romans, and through the study of folklore and later vernacular tales. It isn't until the 11th or 12th centuries that the traditional stories of the Welsh started to be set into writing, and although some of these tales are believed to be of mythic origin with their roots in a distant, Pagan past, none of them identify any of the characters as divinities.

As oral tradition is living tradition, stories tend to evolve to reflect the cultural changes of the people telling the stories; this permits the tales to remain relevant in a way that written work, which is static and reflects a particular moment in time, cannot. It is possible, therefore, that elements of the sacred stories of the Celtic Britons survived in orality, evolving over time into the wonder tales foundational to the legends and lore of their descendants, while becoming interwoven with narrative strata arising from the cultural needs and experiences of subsequent generations.

Seeking Context

A close reading of the Four Branches of *Y Mabinogi* and contemporary tales can assist us in discerning patterns of symbolism and in identifying recurring folkloric motifs. While it is possible to recognize mythic themes in these tales that can be classified as international folk motifs, they cannot give us a clear picture about the origin of the stories, nor enable us to fully understand how the exchange of ideas with other countries may have impacted the growth and evolution of Welsh literary tradition.

Like the rest of *Y Mabinogi,* the Fourth Branch is imbued with layers of symbolism which likely held deeper meaning for its medieval Welsh audience than would otherwise be apparent to modern readers. The present-day study of these stories recognizes brief textual references to other lore - the significance of which was likely clearly understood by their contemporary audiences - but which leave us with only maddening glimpses into what may have been a more expansive corpus of story tradition.

Additionally, in mythological and folkloric studies we recognize a phenomenon known as *diachronism;* it is a mechanism through which tales unconsciously exhibit the cultural and historical trappings of the time in which it is written, even when presenting a story that consciously occurs in a different time period. This phenomenon is present throughout *Y Mabinogi,* and is a critical key for coming to a deeper understanding of the Fourth Branch.

Identifying aspects of medieval culture that permeate the Four Branches and other Welsh tales redacted in this period assists us in reading these stories from the perspective of its contemporary context, rather than only with the cultural bias of modern eyes. It is this modern filter which contributes to the harsh judgement of Blodeuwedd's actions in the Fourth Branch based upon a surface reading of the tale; however, there is much more happening than readily meets the eye. Further, once we have identified the medieval elements of the tales, what remains often contains the mythic remnants of earlier traditions - something of particular importance to modern Neo-Pagans.

The Rights of Women

Scholars believe that much of the tension that underscores the narrative of the Fourth Branch is a reflection of social changes in the status of women in medieval Wales. It contains a mythic resonance that has encoded the memory of a power struggle between the rights of women and men, particularly as it concerns matters of kinship, marriage, and inheritance.

It is possible that some Celtic cultures may have practiced matrilineal inheritance - where titles and property were passed down through the mother line - at some point in their histories. Suggestive evidence that the Pictish tribes of Northern Britain were matrilineal, for example, can be found in Irish chronicles, the Pictish king-lists, and in Bede's *Ecclesiastical History*. We can also find traces of this practice in Welsh, Irish, and Breton myths and legends, even though it is not reflected in any known law code or historical treatise. Whereas matriliny was not practiced in medieval Wales, it is clearly present in the Fourth Branch and elsewhere in *Y Mabinogi*, a fact which seems to further validate the belief that the tales of the Four Branches are of much older origin than their medieval redactions, potentially having persisted in oral tradition since pre-Christian times.

Matronymy, where lineage is identified through the giving of the mother's name, tends to be present in cultures that practice matriliny. Several of the characters in the Fourth Branch are the Children of Dôn, all of whom have matronyms; this includes Gwydion fab ("son of") Dôn, Gilfaethwy fab Dôn, and Arianrhod ferch ("daughter of") Dôn. Dôn was an ancestral figure who may have been a mother Goddess cognate to the Irish Danu, who herself was the progenitor of the similarly matronymic Tuatha Dé Danann - the People of the Goddess Danu. Dôn's brother is Math fab Mathonwy, who may also have a matronym, although we do not know the gender of Mathonwy; ostensibly, Math rules Gwynedd as the head of the matriline.

Perhaps it is the practice of matronymy which underscores

the first of Arianrhod's *tynged* - that her son not have a name save one that she herself gives to him; by giving him a name, she would thereby be acknowledging his place in the matriline. It is evidence of the power of Mother Right to name her child that Arianrhod could place this *tynged* to begin with - an authority so strong that its binding power could not be broken by Gwydion or Math even with all of their magic.

Aside from matronymy, matriliny is most directly illustrated through the concept of inheritance passing through the sister's son. Math himself has no children, which is not problematic as his heir is Gwydion, his sister's son. Similarly, Gwydion's heir is Lleu, the son of his sister Arianrhod who is the daughter of Dôn. At the end of the Fourth Branch, Lleu is without a wife and children, but the larger issue for the continuity of the House of Dôn is not that he has no children, but that he has no sister.

Cultural shifts tend to be gradual, and it is interesting to note the ways in which the tension arising between matriliny and patriliny seem to have been memorialized in the foundational conflicts of the story of the Fourth Branch. There are several other instances where we can see this tension play out both in direct relationship to Blodeuwedd herself, as well as in the events leading up to her creation.

Co-opting Female Power

The first instance of the masculine imposing itself on feminine in the Fourth Branch can be seen in the person of Goewin, both overtly and subtextually. She serves as Math's footholder, and the narrative tells us that he is required to always have his feet in the lap of a maiden, otherwise he would die. The only exception to this requirement is during times of war. This is a strange requirement, and may potentially represent a *tynged*, or fate, that has been lain upon Math, but we do not know its origin and no explanations are given in the Fourth Branch or other texts.

While it is true that medieval Welsh courts included a

position called the king's footholder, they were invariably male, and seemed to only execute this duty during feasts: "It is right for him to hold the king's feet in his lap from when he begins to sit at the banquet until he goes to sleep, and to scratch the King." (Davies, 2007; 240) Perhaps then, the inclusion of the more fantastic version of the position depicted in the Fourth Branch is intended to be an onomastic myth that explains the presence and function of this person at court.

However, the medieval redactor of this tale was very specific in their word choice when it came to describing the required position of Math's feet - a choice which potentially shifts the significance of Goewin's role in Math's court.

"... this passage describes the position of Math's feet, which are *ymlyc croth morwyn* (literally, "in the fold of the womb of a virgin"). The noun *croth*, often translated as "lap," has the base meaning "womb," "uterus," or "belly. " Also, the word that tends to be translated as "in the fold of," *ymlyc*, is a compound of *yw* (in) + *plyc* (fold, curve), which can mean either "in a fold or curve" or simply "within."... Since Middle Welsh had another, less ambiguous word for lap, *arfet*, and this word appears later in the same text, the ambiguity may be intentional. The phrase *ymlyc croth morwyn* connotes varying degrees of intimate contact with the *morwyn* (virgin), from the more innocent "in the fold/curve of a virgin's belly" or "in the lap of a virgin" to the decidedly risqué "in the groin", "pubic hair of a virgin" or even "within the womb of a virgin" whose hymen remains magically intact." (Sheehan, 322)

This suggests that Math's requirement to have his feet in the "lap" of a maiden may indicate something more than a medieval oddity or *tynged*-based limitation. Perhaps instead, this can be interpreted as a rather pointed symbol of Math's kingship - his right to rule - being dependent on having the feminine principle, quite literally, as its foundation.

Gwydion's trickery sends Math off to a manufactured war so that Goewin could be left behind - and left vulnerable to the betrayal of Gilfaethwy who rapes her in his uncle's bed. When Math returns and discovers what his nephews have done, he responds by telling Goewin: "'... I will take you as my wife,' he said, 'and give you authority over my kingdom.'" This marriage transforms the power structure between the two, turning it into partnership, where before Goewin was held in a subordinate position, with Math's feet literally capping and controlling the female powers of sovereignty, which will be discussed in the next chapter.

The Fourth Branch also contains several undeniably overt, and increasingly aggressive, instances of Math and Gwydion using their magic to claim the female power to create life for themselves. First, the punished Gwydion and Gilfaethwy take turns becoming female animals and bearing children to each other by harnessing the regenerative power inherent in their transformed bodies. Second, catalyzed by Math's magic, Arianrhod spontaneously gives birth to twins when she steps over his rod: one which is born immediately, without spending any time gestating in his mother's womb, and the other which falls from her body, essentially as a fetus. This "small thing" is then incubated in Gwydion's wooden chest until it reaches full term - again, without the need for his mother's body.

Finally, the feminine principle is not required at all for the creation of Blodeuwedd. This last action can also be seen as circumventing the last of Arianrhod's binding power of *tynged*, a final victory over Mother Right. Conjured from the flowers of oak, broom, and meadowsweet, Blodeuwedd is not of the race women currently on the earth, as specified by Arianrhod in her third destiny, and so Lleu is able to fully step into his manhood by taking a wife.

Whatever the subtextual symbolism or overt actions of the

characters may once have meant, the patriarchy reveals itself in this myth. The attainment of a wife is part of a checklist required for manhood, and as we see in this story, often has nothing to do with the wants or needs of the woman herself. With this in mind, an understanding of Welsh marriage laws is critical to a deeper understanding of the Fourth Branch.

On Marriage

The *Cyfraith Hywel - The Laws of Hywel Dda* - was an early codification of Welsh law named for King Hywel the Good, who ruled Wales in the 10th century CE. These Celtic laws - with similarities to the Brehon laws of Ireland and which reflected the traditions of the Brythonic kingdoms of the Old North - were used to govern Wales until the final English conquest in the late 13th century. Although never specifically stated, the guiding principles of these laws can be found in each of the Four Branches, and reflect the cultural standards and social mores of Wales in the Middle Ages.

The *Cyfraith Hywel* specifically addressed issues of marriage, dowry, divorce, and inheritance. While by no means equal to men in medieval Wales, women of the time did enjoy some broader rights than did contemporaneous women in other countries; they were able to divorce their husbands, remarry if they so chose, receive monetary compensation for infidelity and physical mistreatment by her husband, and could leave a marriage with the full return of her dowry before seven years have passed, after which a fair and equitable division of wealth between the two parties is proscribed.

There are several points of marriage law that are key to our understanding of the Fourth Branch. First, it must be understood that "... a woman must be a free consenting party to her marriage and could not be disposed of against her will ... there was no selling of a woman in marriage." (T.P. Ellis, 124) We see several marriages occur in *Y Mabinogi* that reflect this law.

- Rhiannon and Pwyll wed in the First Branch, and while Rhiannon is being compelled to marry by her father, she is able to choose her own husband.

- In the Second Branch, a political marriage is brokered between Britain and Ireland, and Branwen's family negotiates on her behalf.

- In the Third Branch, we see Rhiannon's son Pryderi suggest a marriage between his now-widowed mother and his friend Manawydan, brother to Bran and Branwen and rightful heir to the throne of Britain. It may seem odd for a son to be playing matchmaker for his mother, but this too is a reflection of medieval Welsh culture. Women were considered to be under the legal guardianship of their fathers while unwed, of their husbands while married, and of their sons when widowed. Note, however, that even here, Rhiannon must give her consent to enter into a union with Manawydan.

It is notable that we do not see Blodeuwedd give consent to her marriage to Lleu in the Fourth Branch. Even if we assume that she has given consent "off stage," as Branwen appears to have done, as a literal newborn, would Blodeuwedd have even possessed the understanding or capacity required to make such a choice? Further, unlike Branwen, she has no family to negotiate the terms of the marriage on her behalf. She has been created specifically for the purpose of being Lleu's wife, and since her creator is Gwydion, Lleu's uncle, it is clear that his priority is to see his nephew wed - not to advocate on his creation's behalf. And so, Blodeuwedd is married the same day she steps into the world. She is locked into this fate; it is, indeed, her very purpose. And yet, it is this very lack of consent which may have stood out to the contemporary medieval audience, leading them to consider that the marriage between Lleu and Blodeuwedd may not have been proper or legal.

Keeping the issue of consent in mind, there is another key to understanding Blodeuwedd's actions in the Fourth Branch, and it concerns the fact that there were nine forms of legal marriage recognized by Welsh law. These were known as *nau kynywedi teithiauc* or the "nine rightful couplings." Each type of union provided different degrees of economic protection for the women involved. This protection depended upon the economic status of both partners - whether their individual endowments were equal or unequal, and if unequal, which of the two possessed greater wealth - as well as the marriage process itself. From these nine, scholar T.M. Charles-Edwards identified four main types of legal marriage, in decreasing order of status:

- Type One - Unions by gift of kin.
- Type Two - Unions not by gift of kin, but with the consent of the kin and of the woman herself.
- Type Three - Unions to which the woman's kin do not consent, but to which the woman herself does.
- Type Four - Unions to which neither the woman nor her kin consent.

The marriage of Blodeuwedd and Lleu appears on the surface to be of the first type, a union by gift of kin; however, we have already discussed the issue of Blodeuwedd having no family to speak for her. Type Three marriages do not require the consent of kin, and one such form of legal marriage was called *llathlud twyll* - a false or secret elopement. Very specific conditions needed to be met in order for the *llathlud twyll* to be considered a legal union:

Whoever sleeps with a woman for three nights from the time when the fire is covered up until it is uncovered the next day, and wishes to repudiate her, let him pay her a bullock worth twenty pence and another worth thirty and another worth sixty. And if he takes her to house and holding, and she is with him until the end of the seven years, he shares with her as with a woman who had givers. (Owen and Jenkins, 191)

Seem familiar? It is this very scenario which plays out in the Fourth Branch, when Blodeuwedd asks Gronw to stay with her for three nights; he does so, thereby meeting the requirements for *llathlud twyll*. Adding this to the question of the legality of her marriage to Lleu because she is not shown giving consent, it is possible that medieval audiences would have clearly understood what modern readers without knowledge of Welsh marriage laws from the middle ages would not: that she made a true and legal union with Gronw. From a legal standpoint, at least, this casts Blodeuwedd's adultery in a new light.

In addition to never being shown giving consent to her marriage, Blodeuwedd does not even speak in the Fourth Branch until she awakens to her own sense of agency when she falls in love with Gronw. When at last the narrative shows her speaking with her husband, she does so through the filter of his expectations - the demure, simple wife whose concerns center upon his well-being. Using the tools available to her - her beauty, her perceived simplicity, her "feminine wiles" - to accomplish her aims, one can almost see her looking up at Lleu through her eyelashes when she asks him to stand on the edge of the bath later on in the story. It is almost farcical watching Lleu fall prey to her deceit; he believes her to be completely without guile, and never dreamed she would - or even could - throw off her programming.

In the end, it is likely that Blodeuwedd's literary function was to serve as a cautionary example for the tale's medieval audience. Her story illustrates that nothing good comes of women seeking to change their circumstance, especially when it goes against the status quo. Conformity is safe, stable, and unquestionably expected. The perfect woman is one who is beautiful, compliant, and silent. One who has agency, like Arianrhod, is actively undermined throughout the narrative, and negative authorial judgment of her actions is clearly expressed. Further, women's sexual agency is condemned as a destructive force needing to be managed in order to preserve order.

However, when we look even deeper into the symbolic elements of the story, bypassing the medieval layers of the tale, we find an unmistakable mythic residue that appears to reflect an even older dynamic, having to do with the Sovereignty of the land and the forces of nature itself.

Chapter 3

Goddess of Sovereignty

Having examined the cultural underpinnings of the Fourth Branch and explored the potential significance of the story from the perspective of its contemporary medieval audience, it is clear that there is more to Blodeuwedd's tale than meets the modern eye. But if she is not simply an example of the literary motif of the Unfaithful Wife, who is Blodeuwedd? What may she have originally represented? Had she formerly been a deity? It is my belief that the answer can be found by investigating a common motif in the lore and legends of Celtic lands: the female figure who represents the sovereignty of the land.

Sovereignty and the Sacred Landscape

Sovereignty Goddesses are one of the most well-attested Celtic divinity types, and she can be found in Irish, Welsh, and Arthurian myths and legends. Originally a tutelary deity who is the embodiment and protector of her land, she tests potential candidates to determine their worthiness to be granted rulership over the region or country which is in her keeping. Reflecting cultural changes over time, literary depictions of Sovereignty shifted as well, transitioning from a clearly-identified divine figure, to an Otherworldly queen subtextually embodying the sovereignty of the land, to something wholly symbolic or allegorical, such a magical cauldron or the Holy Grail.

This evolution of Sovereignty can make it challenging to identify her presence in later tales, but it is not impossible. As we explore the characteristics of the Sovereignty Goddess motif, it is important to keep in mind that not every powerful female figure in Celtic lore and mythos may have once been considered a Sovereignty figure - or, indeed, a divinity. Since no extant tale from Welsh tradition directly identifies any of the characters as Gods, we must be especially discerning in making these claims as well. There are certain clues that can be found in myth and folklore - including the meaning of names and their etymologies, the presence of linguistic honorifics in naming conventions, syncretism with Roman deities, attendant symbol sets, recognizable literary motifs, and so on - that can help us in the quest to determine which characters may once have been considered divine. (A detailed exploration of this process can be found in another book I wrote for this Pagan Portals series by Moon Books - *Rhiannon: Divine Queen of the Celtic Britons*).

In the case of the personification of the Sovereignty of the land, we are looking at an established international folk motif (Z116 in the seminal collection and classification system of literary mythemes called the *Thompson Folk Motif Index*). Studying the tales where this motif is present reveals several characteristics that can be useful for the identification of sovereignty figures:

1. *Sovereignty and the Land.* She is associated with a specific region of land which is in her care and under her protection. She is empowered to confer rulership over that land to a candidate she deems worthy.

2. *Sovereignty and Liminality.* She is often found at liminal times or in liminal places, especially near wells, rivers, and other bodies of water. These thresholds indicate the presence of the Otherworld, which overlies and overlaps with our world in these in-between places, and underscore the mystical energy of the Sovereignty figure. This association with the Otherworld at the very least serves to identify the Sovereignty figure as Other - a fey creature or land spirit - and potentially signifies that she may have once been considered divine. This liminality is also present in her role as psychopomp - one who facilitates

the transition of a spirit from one state of being to another.

3. *Sovereignty and the Hunt.* An encounter with sovereignty is often presaged in the narrative by a hunt - especially of a stag, which is often white.

4. *Sovereignty as Tester of Potential Kings.* She, or a proxy symbol such as a magical cauldron, tests the worth of potential kings and chieftains to determine their fitness to rule.

5. *Sovereignty and the Sacred Marriage.* She enters into a sexual union - a sacred marriage or *hieros gamos* - with her chosen champion; it is through this act that sovereignty over the land is granted to the man she finds worthy, thereby binding his fate with that of the land. This union can be literal or symbolic.

6. *The Withdrawal of Sovereignty.* She has the power to rescind sovereignty if the king becomes ill or injured, if he rules unjustly, or - in some cases - in accordance with seasonal or annual considerations. This may be seen as an extension of her role as the protector of the land, which also accounts for her common presentation as a martial figure.

7. *Sovereignty as Shape Changer.* She has the ability to change her form, typically testing the candidate in the form of a fearsome hag, and transforming into a beautiful young woman after sexual union with the new king has been achieved. These shifts in form are usually seen as a reflection of the status of the relationship between the king and the land. She often reverts to a hag when the king has lost the right to rule and a new king is needed.

It is important to note that while these are the general criteria for identifying a sovereignty figure, some of these characteristics become more symbolic over time, making aspects of them more difficult to locate in the context of a story's narrative. Further, not every characteristic may be present in later materials, requiring us to be a little looser with our criteria when assessing these tales.

Types of Sovereignty

There are two major forms of the Sovereignty motif that we can identify in myth and legend:

1. *Aperiodic Sovereignty,* where the king or chieftain retains the blessings of Sovereignty so long as his body is whole and his actions are righteous. This can be characterized as a spatial relationship that endures while balance is maintained between the land and those who live upon it, represented by the actions and vitality of their king.

2. *Periodic Sovereignty,* where the leader's right to rule lasts only for a pre-defined span of time. This can be characterized as a temporal relationship between the land and the personification of natural forces that maintains its own balance through the dynamic of seasonal rhythms.

Although it is far more common to see annual or seasonal kingship in the mythos of the Mediterranean and the Near East, the motif is also present in Celtic lands, albeit in more symbolic or subtextual forms.

Blodeuwedd as Sovereignty Goddess

With all of this in mind, let us evaluate Blodeuwedd's story in the Fourth Branch to see if she exhibits the fundamental characteristics that have come to be associated with the figure of Sovereignty.

1. *Sovereignty and the Land.* Unique in Celtic lore, Blodeuwedd is a woman created out of flowers by magic. While she is not stated to be directly associated with a particular territory, she was made from the flowers of oak, broom, and meadowsweet; perhaps these components were harvested from the land that Lleu would come to rule.

2. *Sovereignty and Liminality.* In Celtic legends, the inclusion of threshold times and places signal the presence of the Otherworld even if this is not directly stated in the narrative. While Blodeuwedd's initial entrance into the tale does not occur in an identifiably liminal space, her conjuration by magic connects her with Otherworldly energies. Many significant events in the tale take place at boundary places and near bodies of water, symbolizing that the Otherworld is near. For example, the deaths of Lleu and Gronw occur on the banks of the River Cynfael, and the drowning of Blodeuwedd's maidens and her subsequent transformation into an owl take place in and around Llyn Morwynion.

3. *Sovereignty and the Hunt.* Before the creation of Blodeuwedd to fulfill the third *tynged* placed upon Lleu by Arianrhod, he obtains his name from his mother in defiance of her first *tynged* by symbolically participating in a wren hunt - an act that establishes his royal candidacy (see Chapter 4). Further, when we are introduced to the character of Gronw, he is engaged in a boundary-crossing stag hunt that bled over from his own lands onto those of Lleu. Immediately after he kills and dresses the stag (on the bank of the River Cynfael at dusk - a potent threshold place at a threshold time), he is offered the hospitality of

Blodeuwedd's hearth, and during the feast she provides him, they fall in love.

4. *Sovereignty as Tester of Potential Kings.* Except, perhaps, for the test of trust where Blodeuwedd asks Lleu to stand in the tableau she sets up for him on the banks of the Cynfael, his primary testing comes from his mother, Arianrhod. Only when he had earned his name and the right to bear weapons, and had taken a non-human woman to wife would he be fit to rule. One could argue that the *tynged* that Arianrhod placed upon Lleu were a set of tests intended to catalyze his growth into manhood - and, perhaps, his divinity. On the other hand, the challenge of Blodeuwedd for Gronw to remain with her for three nights, as well as her request that he create the spear that should have been impossible to make (as it was forbidden to work the forge on Sundays during mass), could represent his testing at her hands.

5. *Sovereignty and the Sacred Marriage.* It was only after he wed Blodeuwedd that Lleu was given rulership over the cantref of Dinoding. Similarly, it was only after Gronw "killed" Lleu with his "impossible" spear that he was able to wed Blodeuwedd and could assume rulership over Lleu's lands, adding them to his own.

6. *The Withdrawal of Sovereignty.* The Fourth Branch does not give any reason for Blodeuwedd shifting her loyalty from Lleu to Gronw, other than her having fallen in love with the neighboring lord. The narrative describes Lleu as a just and beloved ruler over his lands, and before he was struck by Gronw's spear, he was healthy and whole. However, the "love triangle" of Lleu, Blodeuwedd, and Gronw is a typical characteristic of tales featuring the

sovereignty motif where kingship is related to seasonality. The parallels that mark the reversal of fortune between the two men - each dying, in turn, by the same method, each at the hands of the other at a place of liminality - is further evidence of Blodeuwedd's role as a seasonal Sovereignty figure.

7. *Sovereignty as Shape Changer.* Like other Sovereignty figures, Blodeuwedd undergoes a change in form during the course of her tale. While this shift does reflect the status of her partnership with her chosen champion, it indicates something different than the more common formula of Sovereignty presenting as a hag or as a beautiful maiden, depending upon the degree to which the king is in balance with the land. Instead, both Blodeuwedd's form - and her very name - changes in the Fourth Branch, potentially as a reflection of which of her two suitors she is currently favoring.

Not only do I believe Blodeuwedd meets the criteria to be classified as a Sovereignty figure, I further believe her to be an example of a periodic, or seasonal, Sovereignty Goddess. Let us explore this motif further.

Seasonal Sovereignty

In general, we can see that Sovereignty serves as a threshold through which a change in status can occur; she is a bridge that connects two opposing states of being. She is empowered to grant a king the right to rule, and holds the ability to rescind that right as well. When the king is united to the land by mating with Sovereignty, the status of the land is a reflection of his rulership: it thrives when he is a righteous leader and is physically whole, and it declines in response to any violation of right leadership or in the presence of any physical failings in the health of the king.

This change in the condition of the land, shifting in turn from fertile to fallow, can also be observed as part of the seasonal round as the earth moves from summer to winter and back again. Concern for the turning of the seasons is a feature of any agrarian society, and it appears to play an important role in the folk practices and lore of Wales, England, and Ireland. Seasonal festivals are especially keyed into the transitional periods between summer and winter, as well as the liminal threshold which marks the passage from the old year to the new.

The interplay between summer and winter is a common motif in many medieval tales, and it reveals a pattern of polarities that has its analogues in the dualities of light and darkness, order and chaos, abundance and the Wasteland, and so on. The threshold places that facilitate the transition from one state to another hold great power, and we see these boundaries manifest as fords and rivers between territories (such as those between this world and the Otherworld, as well as those between kingdoms), as transitional times of day (sunset and sunrise), as feast days which mark the shift between seasons (1st November/Calan Gaeaf and 1st May/Calan Mai), and as annual battles occurring every year - sometimes every year and a day, with that additional day perhaps representing a time outside of time.

These thresholds are associated with boundary crossings of many kinds: supernatural events take place, the natural order of things is circumvented or undergoes a reversal, and some kind of threat or dangerous situation reveals itself. Boundaries between territories - like those between years and between seasons - are lines along which the supernatural intrudes through the surface of existence.

Just as a would-be-king seeks to obtain sovereignty over the land, so do the seasons seek sovereignty over the year in their turn; as both types have an impact on the fecundity of the land, perhaps these dualistic struggles can be said to hold common resonances as they fulfill similar functions. When it comes to the more common aperiodic Sovereignty motif, the status of the land serves as a reflection of the king's fitness to rule. When he is in balanced relationship with Sovereignty, the land flourishes, but when he is out of balance because of illness or unrighteousness, the land experiences challenges like war or famine. With the seasonal Sovereignty motif, however, we see the duality express itself as romantic rivals in the love triangle which characterizes this interplay; one rival exhibits characteristics of the Solar Hero motif, and the other holds correspondence with the Otherworldly Champion archetype.

The rivals battle each other at points of liminality – either in threshold places or at boundary times, or both – and they do so seeking the hand of the maiden who represents Sovereignty. This rivalry differs from the aperiodic Sovereignty motif because it features reversals in status between the two suitors, with their fates often mirror images of each other; one falls from prominence as the other rises, usually occurring at appointed times and in transition places. The representative of Sovereignty favors each champion in turn, and in the mold of the classic Sovereignty figures, not only serves to test the rivals but often is an active participant in the other's fall. In the context of this seasonal allegory, therefore, the Sovereignty figure acts as the pivot around which the year turns, granting her favor to one suitor then the other in succession.

The symmetry of the reversals suggest that something deeper is occurring.

Let us now look at the archetypal characteristics often exhibited by the rivals that complete the love triangle, the figures I have come to identify as the Solar Hero and the Otherworldly Champion.

The Solar Hero is an archetypal force that is in alignment with the energies of order. He is usually, but not always, the protagonist of the tale and is seen as a representative of the Light and all that corresponds with it: sun and sky, summer, the Light Half of the year, daytime, law and order, knowledge, skill, domestication, growth, fertility, agriculture, human society, and this World. His symbols include: eagles, oak trees, lightning, light and daytime, white, and gold.

The Otherworldly Champion, in contrast, is an archetypal force that is in alignment with the energies of disorder. He is usually, but not always, the antagonist of the tale, and is seen as a representative of the Dark and all that corresponds with it: moon and earth, winter, the Dark Half of the year, nighttime, chaos and reversal, wisdom, magic, the wild, decay, death, hunting, the law of nature, and the Otherworld. His symbols include: stags, alder trees, darkness and night, black, and silver.

We will explore how this rivalry plays out in the next chapter.

Llech Ronw

I bring this offering
To the Dark Lord and the Bright
To the nexus of changes
The threshold between
The resolution of the irreconcilable
That heals what has always been whole

The old order must ever fade away
 To herald that which comes
 To lay a pathway for what is new
 To travel along the ley lines of life's eternal strand
Twisting and endless, spun by the spindle-bones of death
Until the leaves fall, carpeting the wood with deepest red
Both womb-blood and placenta
To birth the returning king

This, then, is Sovereignty's gift
Sovereignty's lesson
Sovereignty's price

The balance of time, poised on a razor's edge
Makes room for the offering
 the oath
 the opening
The whole and holey
Holy stone

The body of the maiden, he pierces it
Breaking through the blue-grey slate
The shuddering slab of protection
The fear-wrought shield of doubt
Tombstone and gravestone and memory's marker
Where lovers unite and

Warriors fight and
Eagles take flight

The queen awaits him on the other side
First mourning, then knowing that
Like that first morning
They are thrice united, but all too soon parted
Until she returns to him on owl's wings
While he returns a stag of seven tines,
Dark god
Dark wood
Dark eyes
And then, they are one
On the banks of the Cynfael River

And in that moment of balance
He slips through her threshold -
And a new king is crowned... and crowning.

Chapter 4

Love Triangles and Seasonality

The struggle between night and day, between winter and summer, between this world and the Otherworld can be seen re-enacted by the contest between an Otherworldly Champion and a Solar Hero for the favor of the representative of Sovereignty. Just as the seasons turn through the portals of transition places, and the night changes into day, so too does the Sovereignty of these times and places switch champions whom she favors to rule in turn.

There are many examples of love triangles in Celtic and Arthurian tales which contain aspects of seasonality and sovereignty, "invoking an extremely old mythologic structure: 'the eternal triangle' involving the old king, the new king, and the goddess of sovereignty."(Parker, 122) Here are several examples which illustrate that the theme is common enough to warrant its own literary motif, and which serves to strengthen the notion that the events in the latter half of the Fourth Branch is an example of this motif.

Gwythyr, Creiddylad, and Gwyn

Culhwch ac Olwen features a love triangle which has very suggestive seasonal associations, and is directly tied into the liminal festival of Calan Mai, the transition point between winter and summer. In this tale, two members of Arthur's court, Gwythyr ap Greidol and Gwyn ap Nudd, are rivals for the hand of the maiden Creiddylad. The narrative tells us that the maiden "went off" with Gwythyr, but Gwyn abducts her before the two can sleep together. Gwythyr raises an army against Gwyn, but the latter is triumphant, and rather vicious in his victory.

The narrative states of Gwyn that "God has put the spirit of the demons of Annwfyn in him, lest the world be destroyed," suggesting that he rules over them with his fierceness. Gwyn ap Nudd ("White/Bright/ Holy, son of Mist", whose very name suggests liminality) is known elsewhere in Welsh lore as the Lord of the Wild Hunt and Fairy King of Annwn. Gwyn holds a strong association with Calan Gaeaf, the first day of winter and portal into the dark half of the year, as this is the day when he leads the Wild Hunt to gather the souls of the dead and bring them back with him into Annwn. With these correspondences, we can identify Gwyn as the Otherworldly Champion in this triad.

When Arthur hears of the unrest between Gwythyr and Gwyn, he intervenes to make peace between the two men.

> "This is the agreement that was made: the maiden was to be left in her father's house, untouched by either party, and there was to be battle between Gwyn and Gwythyr every May Day forever from that day forth until Judgement Day, and the one who triumphed on Judgement Day would take the maiden." (Davies 2007, 207)

Given his associations with Calan Gaeaf, it is notable that it is on the opposite day, the first day of summer, that Gwyn engages in eternal, annual combat with Gwythyr for the hand of Creiddylad. Gwythyr ap Greidol ("Victor, son of Scorcher") plays the role of the Solar Hero, as his name also seems to suggest, representing the light half of the year. The meaning of Creiddylad's name is uncertain, but it holds the partial potential meaning "heart" or "center" - which would support her role as the representative of seasonal sovereignty in this triad, the core around which the succession of the seasons turn.

Trystan, Esyllt, and March

The fragmented Welsh tale *Trystan ac Esyllt* features a love triangle between Trystan, Esyllt, and King March; the story contains clear seasonal symbolism, and once more it is Arthur who negotiates a peace between the romantic rivals. Although married to March, Esyllt fled into the woods with her lover Trystan. Her husband seeks out Arthur to assist him in settling the insult done to him by Trystan. Speaking with both men, Arthur made several attempts to settle the matter to no avail, for neither would agree to give up Esyllt.

Finally, Arthur decreed that Esyllt would be with one of them when the leaves were on the wood, and the other when the leaves were not on the wood; he gave March, as her husband, first choice between the two time periods. March chose the time when the leaves were not on the wood - that is to say, the winter - because the nights were longer. When Arthur reported his choice to Esyllt, she rejoiced and sang the following:

"Three trees are good in nature:
the holly, the ivy, and the yew,
which keep their leaves throughout their lives:
I am Trystan's as long as he lives!"

The narrative here makes it clear which of the two rivals is associated with which half of the year - March chooses the winter, leaving summer to Trystan. However, unlike the eternal combat of Gwyn and Gwythyr, in this tale the matter is settled between the suitors because Esyllt takes advantage of a loophole in Arthur's judgement, which sees her aligned with Trystan the Solar Hero.

Cuchulain, Blaithnat, and Cu Roi

The Tragic Death of Cu Roi mac Dairi is a tale from the Irish Ulster Cycle dating from the 8th or 9th century, CE. The story features a love triangle which early Celtic scholar W.J. Gruffydd argues is the original source for the story of Lleu,

Blodeuwedd, and Gronw. While the two tales have several strong commonalities, Gruffydd's attempt to reconcile the stories forces him to discount too many of the differences in order to support his theory that the Welsh version of the tale is at best incomplete, and at worst, a corruption of what he believed to be the original Irish tale. Although modern scholars discount most of Gruffydd's conclusions, the many parallels between the two stories are undeniable, and if one did not influence the other, then at least it is clear that they hold several narrative themes in common.

In brief, the maiden Blaithnat, whose name means "Little Flower", is in love with the hero Cuchulain. However, she is carried off by Cu Roi, a warrior with magical powers and the ability to alter his shape. Even still, the lovers find opportunity to meet on an island to the west, enjoying a tryst on Samhain. There are several variations of the tale; in one, Blaithnat betrays to her lover the secret of how Cu Roi could be killed. This was an otherwise impossible process requiring the destruction of the apple that contained Cu Roi's soul, which first needed to be retrieved from the body of a salmon that only visited a particular spring once every seven years.

Arthurian scholar Roger Loomis saw a parallel between this tale and that of the onomastic myth of Persephone and Hades, writing:

"When faced with the fact that Cuchulain is commonly regarded as a solar hero, that Blaithnat means "little flower" — that the battle for her possession lasted the great Irish seasonal festival of November 1st to the middle of Spring — can we resist the seasonal implications of the story? Here are the flower maiden, the abduction, and the imprisonments of the maiden in the Otherworld during the winter." (Loomis, 17)

The seasonal elements are present in this story, as are the parallels with the events of the Fourth Branch. Blaithnat plays the role of sovereignty and the land reflects the essence of her current mate; she is with Cu Roi in the winter, and Cuchulain in the summer. It is interesting to note that there is some evidence that the story of Cuchulain's birth suggests that he is an avatar of the Irish god Lugh, a deity whose Welsh reflex is Lleu. (Lindahl, McNamara, Lindow, 418)

Sacred Kingship in the Fourth Branch

Kingly sacrifice and succession through combat are themes that are present in the Fourth Branch of the Mabinogi, and are key motifs to explore in order to understand the subtextual allegory of seasonal Sovereignty present in the tale. With this context in mind, we can reinterpret the events of the Fourth Branch from the perspective of seasonal Sovereignty, weaving together our understandings with evidence from lore.

The rivalry between Lleu Llaw Gyffes and Gronw Pebyr in the Fourth Branch engenders a series of mirrored reversals between the two men; as one falls the other ascends, until their fortunes switch once more. In one of many examples of mirroring between Lleu and Gronw, they both symbolically establish, or at least presage, their sacred kingship through the killing of protected animals associated with royalty; in effect, the animals become the sacrificial proxy for their respective kings.

Lleu as Solar Hero

Lleu establishes his role as the summer king when he strikes the wren which has alighted on Gwydion's ship, thus earning a name from his mother, Arianrhod. The wren is considered king of the birds in many European folk traditions, and regional names for the bird translate to his being the "little king" or the "winter king." The wren, a tiny bird known for its reproductive prowess and which famously makes its nests in or close to the ground, was a symbol of fertility. An honored and protected species in medieval times, it was considered bad luck to harm a wren or disturb its nest. However, seasonal folk practices recorded in the last few centuries around the winter holidays in Wales feature the hunting of the usually-protected wren. The man who captures or kills the wren becomes the new "king" for the year, often playing a primary role in the parading of the bird in a mumming practice thought to confer fertility, and believed to represent the dying of the old year and the bringing in of the new, as light returns after the winter solstice.

It is unknown how far back these wren practices go, and whether they have, as some believe, an origin in some kind of annual sacrifice where the bird has become the proxy for the year king. However, it is possible that folk beliefs concerning the wren's significance may have been known to the medieval audience contemporary with the redaction of the Four Branches, thus infusing Lleu's act with a deeper, contextually understood, meaning. The wren, therefore, may represent the king of the old year or else is the avatar of winter - the dark half of the year. By killing or striking the wren, Lleu becomes the king of the new year, or the avatar of the light half of the year; this is reflected by the name he receives after the act, "Fair One of the Steady Hand." Summer has triumphed over winter, and Lleu takes his place as the Solar Hero.

Gronw as Otherworldly Champion

Gronw signals his role as the Otherworldly Champion in similarly subtextual ways. When he first appears in the Fourth Branch, he is engaged in the hunting of a stag, a motif commonly associated with the pursuit of Sovereignty and which often signals an encounter with the Otherworld. For example, in the First Branch, Pwyll meets Arawn, the king of Annwn, while both are engaged in a stag hunt. Gwyn ap Nudd, similarly, is noted to be in charge of the "demons of Annwn" in *Culhwch ac Olwen*, and is famously known in Welsh lore as the leader of the Wild Hunt and king of *y Tylwyth Teg* - the fair folk.

There may be some significance in the fact that the very day that Lleu leaves his court to visit his uncle Math - and although unclear based on the text, it could well be the first time Lleu has left his own court - is the day we meet Gronw hunting on Lleu's land. In his guise as the Solar Hero, the withdrawal of Lleu from his holdings may represent the departure of the light from the land: the summer leaving to make way for winter.

Lord of the lands neighboring those of Lleu, Gronw completes his hunt on the banks of the River Cynfael, a boundary place, and approaches Blodeuwedd's court at nightfall, a boundary time. Threshold times and places have powerful associations with the Otherworld, and we often see combat with the Otherworld occur in spaces of liminality. An example of this can be found in the First Branch, when Pwyll (in the guise of Arawn) engages in battle with Hafgan, a neighboring Otherworldly king, in the middle of the ford of a river. (As an aside, Hafgan's name means "Summer Song").

Just as with Lleu's killing of the wren, the stag hunt is layered with meaning. Like the wren, the stag appears to have been venerated as a royal proxy for the sacrifice of the king. As with most sacrificial animals, the stag holds a liminal quality, representing both death and life, and its appearance in tales heralded the blurring of the boundaries between this world and the Otherworld.

Because of the periodic shedding of its antlers, the stag is connected to the turning of the seasons. As one of the Oldest Animals enumerated in *Culhwch and Olwen,* the stag may have been considered a mythical ancestor for the Celtic Britons, and its powerful rut may have contributed to its strong association with fertility.

The veneration shown for the wren as a royal bird is paralleled by the chivalrous respect for the stag as a royal animal; during the medieval period, strict game laws were in place in Wales and elsewhere that forbade the hunting of stags to anyone without royal consent.

Rivals and Reversals

With their identities thus established, there are several reversals of fortune between the Solar Hero and the Otherworldly Champion in the Fourth Branch.

1. Lleu Overcomes Arianrhod's *Tyngedau* (Destinies) - Lleu's first reversal of fortune comes when he shifts from having no social status to becoming integrated into society. With Gwydion's help, he gains his name, his right to bear arms, and a wife. Thus, stepping fully into his manhood, Lleu is wed to the lady of Sovereignty and granted rule over a cantref. Summer triumphs as portended when he overcame the wren, a symbol of winter.

2. Gronw Triumphs Over Lleu - The second reversal concerning Lleu occurs when he is felled by Gronw's magical spear, in a place of liminality, on the banks of the River Cynfael. Yet another iteration of reversal can be found here, for this is the place where, earlier in the tale, Gronw killed and dressed the stag he hunted before calling at Lleu's court. Gronw has wrested away the sovereignty from Lleu in the same place Gronw demonstrated his own Otherworldly kingship. Indeed, once Lleu flies away in the form of a wounded eagle — a solar totem which, in this case, some have associated with Lleu's soul — Gronw departs with Blodeuwedd. They sleep together at his court, and Gronw takes lordship over Lleu's lands. Winter has triumphed over summer.

3. Lleu Triumphs over Gronw - The third reversal comes

after Gwydion finds and restores Lleu to his humanity. It takes all of the best physicians in Gwynedd to heal Lleu "before the end of the year." Once he is whole, Lleu seeks recompense from Gronw for all that has transpired. Lleu's demands set up the third reversal, requiring that Gronw "must come to where I was when he threw the spear at me, while I stand where he was. And he must let me throw a spear at him." The two men face each other on the banks of the River Cynfael. Lleu casts his spear at Gronw, killing him. With this final reversal, occurring at the same threshold place where Gronw kills the stag, and where a year later he critically wounds Lleu, the Solar Hero has regained sovereignty over his lands, and the Otherworldly Champion has been sent back into the chthonic darkness. Summer has triumphed over winter once more.

Lleu goes on to rule justly, although no mention is made of his taking another wife; at this point in the tale Blodeuwedd has already been turned into an owl, ostensibly forever. There are several possible explanations for Lleu's lack of a mate, if we rule out authorial negligence or subsequent explanation found in a now-missing tale. One option is that Aranrhod's *tynged* still holds, and Blodeuwedd's transformation has left Lleu without a suitable candidate for marriage, and Gwydion has not created a new one for him. Another option is that Lleu has followed in the footsteps of Gwydion and Math in co-opting female power; as such, he may no longer need Sovereignty's partnership to rule. If this latter is the case, there still appears to be evidence of the old order as Lleu's eventual rule over Gwynedd seems to be a result of matrilineal inheritance.

Although it is not directly mentioned in the text, we see Gwydion, Math's sister's son, acting as Math's heir at the beginning of the Fourth Branch, so we may conclude that Gwydion does become lord of Gwynedd after Math's death.

If this is the case, then it would follow that Lleu, Gwydion's sister's son, would take the throne of Gwynedd as Gwydion's heir. Alternatively, if Lleu is biologically Gwydion's son, as some believe the subtext of the Fourth Branch suggests, perhaps Gwydion has succeeded in what scholars have suggested is the underlying struggle of the Fourth Branch: the new patrilineal order seeking to overwrite matriliny. If so, then Lleu inherits directly from Gwydion, not because Gwydion is his uncle, but because Gwydion is his father. A final option is that the tale is left open-ended because the cycle simply repeats itself; when Lleu is lord, Blodeuwedd returns to her flower aspect, when the reversal happens once more, Blodeuwedd's partnership of Gronw sees her return to her owl form.

Death and Rebirth

Although Blodeuwedd faithfully followed the formula Lleu revealed to her that was supposed to bring about his demise, he did not die, but was transformed into an eagle. This whole narrative sequence is full of symbolic meaning that is worth exploring. This is particularly true when we consider that the three *englynion* that Gwydion sings have been established by scholars as the oldest portion of the Mabinogi, and therefore may represent an encoding of an older religious belief system or ceremonial practice. There are mysteries here worthy of exploration; what follows is just a small dip into a very deep pool.

The forbidden weapon, forged by his rival during taboo times, does not kill him; rather, it turns him into an eagle. This reveals his true nature as a sky god in the Indo-European mold, connecting him with deities like Zeus, Taranis, and Jupiter. It is not surprising, therefore, that Lleu's eagle form is found in the highest branches of an oak tree, another common symbol of sky gods. This is clearly no ordinary tree, as it bears the liminal characteristics of the Otherworld: it grows between two lakes, it bridges sky and glen, it grows in upland ground that is beneath the slope, and it can neither be wetted nor burned.

Because he didn't die when struck by the spear, let us suppose that Lleu underwent a spiritual death instead. Birds are often used to represent the souls of the dead and the spirits of shamans and other ecstatic practitioners who journey between the worlds, such as the Welsh Awenyddion. Flying off in the form of an eagle could represent an ascension of the World Tree - the axis mundi or sacred center - which in Celtic cosmology connects the Three Realms of Sky, Land, and Sea: that which is above, the Future; that which is around, the Present; and that which is below, the Past.

In her role as a Goddess of Sovereignty, Blodeuwedd initiates this process for Lleu - testing his worth by setting up the parameters that see him meet the seemingly impossible circumstances that would bring about his death. By manifesting a place of triple liminality - placing him neither indoors nor outdoors, neither on foot nor on horseback, and on the bank of a river - she has essentially constructed a portal for him that invokes the Otherworld through the sacred power of three.

The top of the tree may represent the Realm of Sky - the dwelling-place of the Gods and the origin of the great cosmic pattern. Perhaps Lleu was working to claim the truth of his divinity there, by integrating the lessons that Arianrhod had set before him, a process somewhat circumvented by Gwydion as he had bypassed all of her *tynged* on Lleu's behalf. Perhaps the creation of Blodeuwedd - which was catalyzed by Arianrhod - ensured that he would have to make the shifts and transformational changes intended by his mother in order for him to truly come into his power.

Whatever the purpose this process may have served, it is clear that Lleu engages in deep healing. He releases what is wounded and rotten, and uses his wings to shake off what no longer serves him, allowing it to fall away to the bottom of the tree, perhaps representing the Realm of Sea - the dwelling place of the ancestors, where the souls of the dead rest and await rebirth. The primal chthonic energy represented by the sow - an animal associated with the Otherworld in *Y Mabinogi* - feeds off Lleu's rotted flesh, a form of theophagy which paves the way for his return.

The *Englynion Gwydion* call Lleu's soul back from the Otherworld to inhabit his human form once more - a rebirth once again facilitated by the magician. Lleu's weakness upon his return is consistent with someone who has been on an intense ecstatic journey. Once strengthened, the twice-born Lleu seeks to regain his lands and his power, and he does so on his own merit - strong, just, and triumphant. He no longer needs his uncle's intervention, and steps into his rule on his own terms, eventually succeeding Math as king of Gwynedd.

It is meaningful for us to look at this sequence from a psychospiritual perspective, as well. Perhaps Gronw represents Lleu's Shadow-self, and the directed intention of the spear, made during sacred times - at the prompting of Sovereignty - represents the unconscious will to initiate change and healing. Certainly, the narrative of the Fourth Branch depicts Gronw as Lleu's opposite in many ways. Where Gronw teaches Blodeuwedd the art of deceit, coaching her in how to extract the necessary information from her husband on how he could be killed, Lleu does not hesitate in his trust of her. Not only does Lleu provide Blodeuwedd with the key to his very undoing, he also willingly gets into the fatal position where the hidden Gronw can cast the spear at him.

Gronw is undoubtedly a shadow dweller: he overstays his time on Lleu's lands, causing Blodeuwedd to invite him to her hall - as is proper, under the rules of hospitality - under the cover of night. He hides behind a hill, so as to ambush Lleu at his moment of vulnerability, and when Lleu regains his strength and challenges his usurper, Gronw continues to hide: first behind offers of monetary compensation, which Lleu rejects; then by asking one if one of his warriors would take the blow from Lleu's spear on his behalf, which no-one accepts; and finally by blaming everything on the wiles of a woman, and asking to hold a slab of stone between him and Lleu. Just as Gronw's warriors are remembered as one of the Three Dishonorable Warbands of the Island of Britain for not standing in for their lord, so is Gronw's cowardice revealed throughout the tale.

But what is cowardice, other than a survival response towards fear… and one of the protective functions of Shadow? If Gronw represents Lleu's Shadow, then this portion of the Fourth Branch may be providing us with a mythic map that guides us in how to face and overcome our Shadow tendencies: by entering the realm of the Unconscious, seeking out the truth of our divine nature, and working to identify and release the outmoded perspectives and ways of being in the world which prevent us from acknowledging the truth of who we are. Proceeding from a center of wholeness rather than one of woundedness allows us to succeed in Sovereignty's challenge, so that we may live from a place of balance and right relationship with both our inner and outer landscapes.

Lady of Darkness, Lady of Light

Recasting the events of the second half of the Fourth Branch in terms of the Seasonal Triangle is the key to unlocking the deeper meaning of the tale, as well as understanding the underlying motivations of its players.

Consigned to literary infamy as the Welsh iteration of the Unfaithful Wife motif, reclaiming the symbolic underpinnings of Blodeuwedd's story liberates her essence and reveals the truth of her sovereign nature - which is, that she represents the Sovereignty of Nature. She is the threshold between daytime and night, the axis around which the wheel of the year turns, the fulcrum that moves the seasons from summer to winter… and back again.

In turn a sun-drenched flower, in time a night-hunting owl, she changes her form to reflect her current sovereign alliance, favoring in turn the Solar Hero and the Otherworldly Champion.

These shifts in form reflect her ability to successfully navigate each realm in turn. What better than a form of flowers to follow the path of the sunlight, drinking in its vitalizing rays to nourish the sweetly-scented fertile potential of the light half?

Who better than a clear-sighted owl to explore the realms of the night - now soaring in star-dappled sky, now stalking her elusive prey - swooping to earth with silent precision to hit her mark with strong, sharp talons?

Two sides of the same nature, she holds the potential of life and rebirth, as well as the sacrifice of death - for life must feed on life.

Lady of Transitions, she illustrates the many changes occurring in the world around us and the space within us. Flowers, once fertilized, become a harvest of fruit and nuts, beans and berries - changing form, transmuting the life-giving energies of the sun into a bounty of food that can feed many. Owls, like all hunters, must take the life of other animals in order to sustain their own. While some flesh must be sustained by flesh, nature maintains a balance. In the animal world, hunters take only what they need, and the deadly accuracy of owls brings a swift end to their necessary prey. All life, in turn, will return to the earth; and even as the energies of the body surrender to the soil, it does so in order to to nurture the next growth of seeds - for even winter must yield to the rebirth of spring.

There is no judgment in the world of light and dark, day and night, summer and winter. The Lady of Sovereignty partners with each in turn, bringing forth the skills and gifts best suited to empower in each circumstance.

Beauty of form, sweetness of demeanor, softness of heart.
Swiftness of wing, sharpness of talon, stillness of death.
Blodeuwedd knows them both.

The Fulcrum and The Balance

Lady of Flowers... of summer... of life.
Lady of Owls... of winter... of death.
Balancing opposites, and opposing imbalance.
Bedding the dawn and birthing the night.
The flower that grows towards the sun
The owl that flies beneath the moon.

She stands at the Threshold
Of initiation... of dying... of rebirth
Summer to Winter, light to dark, day to night
Winter to Summer, dark to light, night to day
She opens and closes and opens again
The door that swings between this world and the Otherworld
Fragrant and feathered psychopomp
She turns the key
She tips the fulcrum
So one may rise and one may fall

Spear into flesh, into stone, into death
Lightning flash of phallic passion
Straddling the river bank
The buck, the cauldron
Not within, nor without
Now this side of the river, now the other
She embraces each lover anew
While laying the old one down on the river bed

By two names you will know her

One that is flowers
One that appears to be flowers -
But is sharp eyed, sharp eared, sharp taloned

She is Lady of the fertile land - the brewer of medicines that
heal, protect, beguile
She is Hunter of the darkest night - the gatherer of flesh, of
blood, of bones
She is a riot of blooms in a meadow
She is a silent winged shadow in the night.

She knows the abundance of summer, the fallowness of
winter.
The warmth of the day, the chill of the night
The vitality of this world, the deathlessness of the Otherworld.
The warrior, the craftsman, and the magician.
The eagle, the wren, and the stag.
The Summer Lord. The Winter King.

The ancient seasonal pantomime playing
Through battles of rivals
Through struggles of lovers
Embedded in legend, in folklore, in memory
Some ancient... some newly-birthed... all timeless

The Oak King and the Holly King
Battling eternally at the twin thresholds
Of the summer and the winter.
One always rising, as the other falls,
Then rises again, to take his rival's place.

But what of the fulcrum, the center?
What of she who grants the gifts of sovereignty to he who
earns by right of battle

He who proves himself worthy to be consort to the land?
To be consort for a season?
Granting rulership over space, and over time...
But only for a time.

She straddles both worlds
And be it through the
Cleft of her vulva, or the hole in the stone,
She initiates. She withdraws. She begins again.
Light to dark to light once more.
Flowers to feathers. Winds to wings.

Sovereign Lady
Lady of Sovereignty
Through her, two halves become whole -
Become Holy.

Chapter 5

The Flower Bride

How does one create a woman? What is the magical formula for calling a Goddess forth from the Otherworld? According to the Fourth Branch, this is how Math and Gwydion undertook to make a wife for Lleu:

> Then they took the flowers of the oak, and the flowers of the broom, and the flowers of the meadowsweet, and from those they conjured up the fairest and most beautiful maiden that anyone had ever seen. And they baptized her, and gave her the name of Blodeuedd*. (Davies 2007, 58)

(Please note: as she is being specifically discussed in her aspect of the Flower Bride, we will refer to her as Blodeuedd in this chapter.)

The redactor of the Fourth Branch took care to be explicit about the flowers included in Blodeuedd's formulary; it is therefore likely that these particular blooms held significance to the contemporary medieval audience, and that they subtextually transmitted information about her nature and character. While scholar W.J. Gruffydd's suggestion - that oak was chosen for the strength of her bones, broom for the yellow of her hair, and meadowsweet for the purity of her white skin - seems very straightforward from a modern perspective, these flowers may have held additional meaning to the medieval Welsh. That none of these plants are in flower at the same time may indicate that there was a temporal component to the magical working, and further underscores the idea that they were deliberately chosen. A deeper exploration of these plants from both a folkloric and medicinal perspective may bring additional insight to broaden our understanding.

Flowers from the Fourth Branch

1. **Oak (*Quercus robur*).** Oak (*dair*) is one of the chieftain trees of the ogham alphabet - a system of writing used in Ireland and parts of Britain, believed to date to at least the 4th century CE - which features trees among the correspondences associated with each letter. In addition to its ogham association with Strength, oak is believed to have been especially sacred to the druids, something reinforced by the etymological link between the Celtic words for both. Stemming from the Proto-Indo-European root words **deru* - which means "tree", and in particular the oak tree (as with *derw*, which is "oak" in Welsh) - and **weid*, which means "to see", we get the Old Celtic words **derwos* ("true") and **wid-* ("to know"). Together, these make the compound word **dru-wid,* which can translate to mean "strong seer" or "true knower" or "one who knows the oak." (https://www.etymonline.com/word/druid)

The famed ritual described by Roman historian Pliny the Elder in his *Natural History* concerns the druids of Gaul cutting mistletoe from the boughs of the sacred oak on the sixth day of the moon. He further states, "Of itself the robur (oak) is selected by them to form whole groves, and they perform none of their religious rites without employing branches of it; so much so, that it is very probable that the priests themselves may have received their name from the Greek name for that tree." (Plin. Nat. 16.95)

In many Indo-European derived cultures, oak trees are sacred to sky and thunder Gods such as Zeus, Jupiter, and Thor. The oak also has a strong association with the motif of the Solar Hero, a correspondence clearly illustrated in the Fourth Branch; it is an oak tree which shelters the wounded Lleu when he is in eagle form - another symbol commonly associated with divinities of sky and thunder. In more recent folklore, the seasonal battle between the Oak King and the Holly King, the Oak King represents the vitalistic power of the increasing Sun which begins to wane after his defeat at midsummer; he is reborn again at midwinter and the days begin to lengthen in response to his return.

Medicinally, oak is a powerful astringent and antiseptic, making it useful to treat wounds, staunch bleeding, and to quell fevers. It can be used as a poultice to draw out infection and inflammation, and has antiviral and antifungal properties. The healing properties of the oak may be another reason the wounded Lleu sought its limbs for shelter.

The addition of oak blossoms in the formula used to create the Flower Bride appears to weave a strong connection between Blodeuedd and Lleu, the Solar Hero she was created to marry. Their inclusion may also reflect a druidic origin of the magics of Math and Gwydion.

2. **Broom (*Cytisus scoparius*).** Broom holds traditional association with the ogham *ngetal*, although Robert Graves and those inspired by his work associate *ngetal* with reed instead. *Ngetal* is an ogham of healing, and can represent both the healer and that which needs to be healed. In folk medicine, broom was used to cool fevers, and was part of the *materia medica* of the Physicians of Myddfai — a world-famous Welsh lineage of healers spanning from medieval times into the early modern period.

Medieval literature often used broom as a descriptor for beauty; we see it directly mentioned to describe Olwen's yellow hair in *Culhwch ac Olwen*, and it may likewise allude to Blodeuedd's hair color in the Fourth Branch. Broom was often included in brides' bouquets, which may also account for its inclusion in Blodeuedd's formula.

Broom is a powerful cleansing herb, both energetically and physically, and it is traditionally used in the making of besoms, as its name suggests. It was used to clear the house on May Day (Calan Mai), a day of seasonal transition between the winter and the summer. A protective herb, broom flowers can be burned to dispel negative influences.

An incredibly useful plant, broom was used to weave baskets and to thatch roofs. Its fibers were spun to make cloth, and the tannins in its bark made it useful for tanning leather. The roots of this common plant act to anchor soil, which helps to prevent erosion, especially in coastal areas. The spindly branches of this shrub shelter wildlife, particularly when is grows as part of a hedgerow.

Broom was famously used in Brittany as a heraldic device, and the English royal house of Plantagenet took the plant's medieval name, *planta genista*, as its own. Traditionally, broom has been used medicinally to treat complaints of the cardiovascular system, as a diuretic, and to induce labor; however, caution should be practiced when taking this herb internally. It should only be used under professional supervision, as poisoning can occur.

3. Meadowsweet (*Spiraea ulmaria*). Also called "bridewort" and "Queen of the Meadow" the intoxicatingly-scented white flowers of the meadowsweet are ubiquitous in the Welsh countryside, and can often be found in boundary places such as hedgerows, ditches, and riverbanks. It was a traditional addition to the bridal bouquet, perhaps because its scent was so seductively sensual. It was also a common funerary herb throughout Wales and Scotland, dating all the way back to the Bronze Age, and perhaps the inclusion of this flower in the making of Blodeuedd presages the role she will play in Lleu's "death." However, considering that it also holds a strong connection with marriage, meadowsweet may have generally represented the transition from one life phase to the next. In Yorkshire, meadowsweet is called "courtship and matrimony"; this is another reflection of the herb's dual nature, as the sweet scent of the flower contrasts with the bitter almond scent of its leaves - just as courtship is joyful while marriage can often turn bitter.

The threshold nature of meadowsweet may account for its

traditional folk use in County Galway, Ireland, where it was believed that placing the blooms overnight under the bed of someone wasting away from contact with the fairy folk would bring them back to health the next morning - although leaving the flowers there for too long could cause the person's death. The flower was considered sacred to Áine, sovereignty Goddess of Munster, who was also revered as a Fairy Queen, and is said to have given the flower its sweet scent. An Irish common name for meadowsweet is *Lus Cuchulainn*, which means "Belt of Cuchulainn." It is said that the legendary warrior's battle fevers could be soothed by meadowsweet baths, and that he would carry the flowers in his belt to keep him from his rages.

According to Grieve, the Druids held meadowsweet in high regard, and counted it as one of their three most sacred herbs, along with vervain and water mint. Said to instill a sense of gladness and peace, meadowsweet flowers were strewn on the floors of houses, and were a popular ingredient in the making of mead and ale. It is possible that its English name comes from the Anglo-Saxon words *mede* ("mead") or *medo-wort* ("honey herb"). The name of the Irish Queen Medb of Connacht means "Mead" or "Intoxicating Goddess", and may also reference her role as a Sovereignty Goddess; there appears to be a strong connection between these two functions. There are hints of mead rituals associated with sovereignty rites in Irish literature, and the idea persists that the mead itself was divine, and is sometimes personified by a Goddess.

In sum, then, the liminal nature of meadowsweet and its transitional qualities - between sweetness and bitterness, between maiden and married woman, between life and death, between rage and calm, between sobriety and intoxication, between this world and the Otherworld - seem to support the idea of Blodeuedd as a Goddess of Sovereignty: she who makes the sacred marriage between the king and the land, and has the power to withdraw her sovereignty - even requiring the sacrificial death of the old king.

Medicinally speaking, meadowsweet contains salicylates, the primary component of aspirin, and so has traditional usage for pain relief and the reduction of fevers. Among its many medicinal uses, it is an excellent anti-spasmodic, and assists with menstrual cramps.

Flowers from *Cad Goddeu*

Cad Goddeu (The Battle of the Trees), a poem from the 14th century *Llyfr Taliesin (The Book of Taliesin)* includes a verse that appears to reference the creation of Blodeuedd by Math and Gwydion, although she is never directly named. This iteration of the tale presents a somewhat different formulary than that found in the Fourth Branch:

When I was made,
Did my Creator create me.
Of nine-formed faculties,
Of the fruit of fruits,
Of the fruit of the primordial God,
Of primroses and blossoms of the hill,
Of the flowers of trees and shrubs.
Of earth, of an earthly course,
When I was formed.
Of the flower of nettles,
Of the water of the ninth wave.
I was enchanted by Math,
Before I became immortal,
I was enchanted by Gwydyon
The great purifier of the Brython

While only three flowers are mentioned in *Y Mabinogi*, *Cad Goddeu* makes several references to the number nine, seeming to imply that there were nine components used in her creation.

The inclusion of "the water of the ninth wave" is a reference to the Otherworld, and is perhaps a subtextual encoding of Blodeuedd's true nature; it was believed that anything beyond the ninth wave of the sea has crossed the boundary between what is known and what is unknown, between this world and the Otherworld. Although the poem does not specify what these nine-formed faculties may have been, instead enumerating general ingredients such as blossoms of the hill and the flowers of trees and shrubs, it does add two more flowers to our list: primrose and nettle.

4. Primrose (*Primula vulgaris*). Primrose blossoms in early spring, and its name - meaning "first rose" - is believed to reflect this, although it is not in the rose family. A yellow flower that often grows in hedgerows, Primrose has associations with May Day, and like other boundary herbs, it is said to grant fairy Sight. It has protective properties, especially when placed over a threshold. In Irish folklore it is said: "Guard the house with a string of primroses on the first three days of May. The fairies are said not to be able to pass over or under this string." The blooms themselves are believed to be keys that open the door to the Otherworld. Touching a fairy stone with a bouquet of primrose can allow one to enter the fairy realms, but if the bouquet contained the wrong number of flowers, bad fortune lay beyond the threshold.

Shakespeare used the term "primrose path" to refer to following a life of pleasure, often without thought of consequence. Primrose was associated with the fertility of hens, and bringing primroses into the home while hens were laying affected the amount of eggs that would hatch; to ensure the most successful hatching, at least thirteen primroses should be brought indoors.

Like broom flower, primrose was used as a descriptor in Celtic legend for beautiful yellow hair. In the Irish tale, *The Wooing of Étaín*, the inhabitants of fairy land are described as having hair "like the crown of the primrose." In the Scottish Hebrides, on the eve of Brigid's Day, girls would create an effigy of a woman from a sheaf of wheat, and decorate it with natural objects including primroses. Called a Bridey Doll, it was placed in a window while the girls feasted alone, and anyone who wished to enter had to ask permission and give a sign of respect to the image in the window.

5. Nettle (*Urtica dioica*). The nettle plant grows wild and abundantly in Britain, and is one of the most commonly used herbs in folk medicine. It is a plant with powerful healing qualities, but has the ability to cause hurt as well — an apt allusion to Blodeuedd's actions in the Fourth Branch. The word "nettle" has its origins in the Anglo-Saxon word *noedl*, which means "needle", and may be a reflection of the plant's traditional use as a textile fiber, which was spun and woven into linen. Alternatively, it may be a reference to the nettle's stinging properties, which is also attested by its botanical name *urtica*, which means "burning." Famous for its sting, the plant is also called "stinging nettle" due to the painful reaction caused by the venom on its hair-like spines when it comes into contact with skin.

"Three nettles in May keeps all diseases away" is an old English saying, reflecting the high regard held for nettle's medicinal properties. Nettles are one of the most nutritious plants known to us, providing a range of necessary vitamins, minerals, and protein, all in a very bioavailable form. Its high iron content assists in the treatment of anemia, and it also has strong anti-hemorrhaging, or hemostatic, properties. It is a powerful antihistamine and an anti-inflammatory herb, especially as concerns the respiratory system; it is used to treat hay fever, sinusitis, and asthma.

Nettle was counted among the nine sacred herbs in Anglo-Saxon folklore, along with plantain, chamomile, mugwort, watercress, chervil, fennel, and crab apple. Nettle was hung around the house or burned in bonfires to protect the household and crops from lightning - an interesting counterbalance to oak, which is the tree most likely to be hit by lightning, and is associated both with Lleu and Blodeuedd. Nettle that was picked on Summer Solstice was especially potent for use in undoing curses. In Scotland, it was believed that nettles harvested on Halloween night and placed in the bedding of someone you fancied would make them fall in love with you.

The positive effect of nettle on both the women's reproductive system and men's virility made it a natural aphrodisiac, and a common component in love spells. However, the dual nature of the herb sees it used both as a method of contraception - a popular folk practice was to place nettle leaves in a man's shoes to prevent him causing pregnancy - and to induce sexual vigor through the process of *urtication* (which is the act flogging a man's genitals with nettle stalks).

Flowers from *Hanes Blodeuwedd*

In his seminal work, *The White Goddess*, 20th century British author and mythologist Robert Graves deconstructs the story of Blodeuedd in the context of his poetic theories, and includes a poem called *Hanes Blodeuwedd*. Having extracted several verses from *Cad Goddeu*, Graves expanded upon them in the writing of his poem, which reads like an alternate translation of the source material:

Not of father nor of mother
Was my blood, was my body.

I was spellbound by Gwydion,
Prime enchanter of the Britons,
When he formed me from nine blossoms,
Nine buds of various kind;

From primrose of the mountain,
Broom, meadow-sweet and cockle,
Together intertwined,
From the bean in its shade bearing
A white spectral army
Of earth, of earthly kind,
From blossoms of the nettle,
Oak, thorn and bashful chestnut –
Nine powers of nine flowers,
Nine powers in me combined,
Nine buds of plant and tree.

Long and white are my fingers
As the ninth wave of the sea.

We can see that in writing his poem, Graves expanded the number of flowers used to create Blodeuwedd from the three mentioned in the Fourth Branch to nine, as suggested in *Cad Goddeu*. Save for the primrose and nettle, which were taken directly from *Cad Goddeu*, there is no indication of where Graves sourced these additional flowers, so we cannot say that these are traditional to Blodeuedd's tale. Graves' additions are: cockle, bean, chestnut, and hawthorn.

6. Cockle. There are several species of plants which bear the common name "cockle", and there isn't any additional information included in the poem to help narrow down which one Graves intended. Perhaps the most likely candidate is White Cockle, also called White Campion (*Silene latifolia*). Containing toxic saponins, white campion has no traditional medicinal usage, however, its roots can be boiled down to release the sudsy properties which saw this plant used as a soap substitute. Aside from this cleansing quality, which connects it to the energetic properties of the canonical broom, white campion has a few other attributes which might explain why Graves included it in his list of flowers for Blodeuedd, particularly as a foreshadowing of her owl form.

Unlike many flowers, white campion does not close its flowers at dusk; instead, it releases a particularly sweet fragrance at sundown, famous for attracting moths as pollinators. It is also infamously bad luck to pick these blooms, and folklore cautions that doing so can result in the death of one's mother. Another common name for this plant is "thunder flower", and children are warned that picking white campion attracts lightning and puts them at risk of being struck. The shell-like bladder of this flower can be squashed between the thumb and forefinger, resulting in a popping sound which may also account for its connection with thunder; this makes for an interesting connection to Blodeuedd, as Lleu has many symbolic resonances with other Indo-European sky Gods - including oak trees and eagles - and many of these divinity types are also associated with thunder. Finally, a type of divination was practiced using white cockle wherein one would ask a question of the flower, and the louder the sound one made when popping the bladder, the more affirmative the answer to the querent's question.

7. Bean. It is hard to say with any certainty what species of bean Graves is referring to here, as there are many. The description in the poem of the "shade bearing white spectral army" at the least may indicate that it is a species with white flowers, which puts it in alignment with some of the other flowers more canonically associated with Blodeuedd. Beans are a staple food stuff around the world as they are excellent sources of protein. However, the consumption of raw or undercooked beans can be fatally toxic, and so there is an underlying menace inherent in the food.

Considering Blodeuedd's role as the Flower Bride, brought forth to be the wife of Lleu, a divine figure associated with light as well as a mythic iteration of the Solar Hero, it is worth noting that a fairly universal quality of bean plants is that they are heliotropic: the leaves tilt and change position in order to follow the daily track of the sun, absorbing as much light as possible. At night, the leaves and flowers close up in the absence of the sun, awaiting the morning to open once more.

8. Chestnut. When it comes to the flowers of the "bashful chestnut", we are faced with several issues. First, Graves does not clarify which of the two types of chestnut trees that grow in the British Isles he is referring to in the poem: sweet chestnut (*Castanea sativa*) or horse chestnut (*Aesculus hippocastanum*), and second, neither of these trees are native species. The Romans are believed to have introduced sweet chestnut to Britain, the nuts of which they ground into a course flour meal, and so the Britons would have been familiar with the tree from around the first century CE onward. The long yellow catkins of the flowering sweet chestnut tree are visually similar to the flowers of oak and nettle, establishing at least a symbolic connection to other flowers included in the more canonical list.

The horse chestnut, on the other hand, was brought to the British Isles from Turkey in the latter half of the 16th century. While it was known to Graves, who was born outside of London in 1895, it is not a tree with deep folkloric tradition in Britain, and is best known for the use of its nuts in the game of conkers. However, the equine associations of the horse chestnut tree are somewhat striking; its nuts are fed to horses as medicine for coughs, and its leaves make a horseshoe-shaped scar when they fall off their twigs. Perhaps these symbolic resonances with horses - that powerful representation of Celtic Sovereignty - may account, at least in part, for Graves' association of the flowers of the horse chestnut tree with Blodeuedd - if, indeed, this is the tree he intended.

9. Hawthorn (*Crataegus spp.*). Hawthorn (*uath*) is another tree featured in the ogham alphabet. It is a boundary tree often found in hedgerows or growing over holy wells, and through it, the Otherworld can be accessed. This may account in part for its association with Calan Mai, that doorway between the Dark and Light Halves of the year. Hawthorn is also known as the May Tree or May Bush, and in some traditions, the transition into summer is not marked by a calendar date, but by the flowering of the hawthorn trees.

Its white blossoms feature in many folk practices associated with May Day. When one goes "a-maying", for example, one is ostensibly gathering hawthorn blossoms with which to decorate the outside of the home, but this "gathering of flowers" may have had some sexual connotations as well. In some areas of Britain, folk celebrations of May Day include the selection of a young, unmarried woman as May Queen and crowning her with a wreath of flowers; it is not hard to see a reflection of Blodeuedd in this practice, but no direct connection can be made, other than that both are representatives of the fertile energies of Spring.

* * *

It is interesting to note that while the four flowers added by Graves are not found in any original source material, they nevertheless hold energetic resonance with those named in the Fourth Branch and *Cad Goddeu* in several ways. It is worth examining the qualities of a few of these additions in order to get a sense of why Graves may have chosen the flowers that he did to include in *Hanes Blodeuwedd*. All of Graves' flowers are either white like meadowsweet, or yellow like broom and oak blossoms; perhaps these are allusions to Blodeuedd's appearance, as pale white skin and blonde hair is a common beauty standard in Celtic literature.

An energetic that appears to be missing from the flowers in the Fourth Branch, but is present in *Cad Goddeu* and Graves, is that of a dangerous beauty. Blodeuedd's dual nature - as dutiful wife and betraying lover, as Lady of Flowers and Night-Hunting Owl - is represented by the inclusion of hawthorn and nettle in the herbal formula that creates her. The hawthorn tree sports sharp, spiny thorns as protection, while the nettle plant is famous for its sting. Both plants have powerful healing qualities, and yet both can cause injury as well — an apt representation of the two sides of Blodeuedd, and perhaps the motivation for including these flowers in alternative, and more modern, accounts of her creation.

Flowers of Devotion

For those dedicated to Blodeuwedd, or who want to form a relationship with her, the gathering together of her flowers to create an incense to burn or an energetic elixir to take is a meaningful act of devotion. The majority of these flowers require that you harvest them for yourself as most are not sold commercially. The fact that it may take years to assemble all of the components is a reflection of that devotion, and will make the floral mixture, once complete, a worthy offering to the Goddess.

As you obtain them, spend some time working with each of the flowers in turn. Meditate upon each one, seeking out their connections to Blodeuedd. Consider doing some in-depth research of their medicinal, folkloric, and energetic qualities. When you feel ready to make the mixes, begin with making a blend with the three flowers mentioned in the Fourth Branch, the "canonical" blooms, and then start looking for all nine flowers if you feel so drawn. Once you have all of them, compare the three-flower blend to the one with nine flowers to feel out the differences — and similarities — between the two blends. Then, going forward, use the one with which you resonate the most as you work with this beautiful and complex divinity.

New from the Old

When I first undertook a study of Blodeuwedd's flowers several decades ago, I wrote a devotional chant that references all nine blooms; because of this I named it *Hanes Blodeuwedd* after Graves' poem.

I am the stinger and the healer (nettles)
I am the cup of mountain's dew (primrose)
I am the guardian of the sunlight (oak)
I am the Maybush in full bloom (hawthorn)
I am the sweet brush cliff-side cleanser (broom)
I am the fruit found deep inside (chestnut)
I am the feeder of the masses (bean)
I am the dowry of the bride (meadowsweet)
I am the friend of womankind (cockle)
I am the Nine in me combined

Hanes Blodeuwedd

Jhenah Telyndru

The Owl

The significance of Blodeuwedd's transformation into an owl is complex, reinforcing the notion that cultural context is key to the understanding of myth and folklore, and demonstrating that meaning can shift over time as a mirror of social change.

Early Celtic Culture

We can trace the owl's importance to Celtic culture to the earliest periods, as far back as the 5th century BCE. Owls were a common motif in early Celtic art; their forms ranged from full-body, naturalistic statuettes discovered with grave goods to decorative embellishments of their faces on torcs, fibulae, and votive cauldrons. Stylized owls, featuring large round eyes and disk-like faces, are often depicted emerging from the heads of humans, lions, or rams. In another variant, owl faces are formed by the merging heads of two identical animals. An illustrative example of this is found on a bronze vessel from the 4th century BCE, depicting an owl's face created by the overlapping heads of two horses that are facing each other.

Images of birds perched upon, or emerging from, human heads is well-attested in Celtic art and artifacts. A figure on the famed Gundestrup Cauldron, dating to approximately the 2nd century BCE, is depicted wearing a helmet with a bird mounted on it, and we have also discovered real-life examples of these helmets believed to have been worn by Celtic warriors. The most remarkable example of this type of helmet was found in Ciumesti, Romania. Dating back to the 3rd century BCE, the helmet's crest is a bronze bird of prey with outstretched and articulated wings that would flap up and down in response to the movement of its wearer.

Not surprisingly, birds of prey and carrion birds are often associated with divinities of war. In Celtic cultures, ravens and crows are especially linked with martial Goddesses like the Irish Morrigan and the Gaulish Cathubodua. Often, these deities of war are also Sovereignty Goddesses, for their main function is to ensure the survival of the land, and as such, they are responsible both for its fertility and its defense. A helmet decorated with an animal effigy associated with a war goddess, therefore, may have served a dual purpose as well: to frighten opponents on the field of battle, as well as to invoke the protection and power of the Goddess herself for the wearer and their comrades in arms.

Overall, it appears that owls were held in high regard by continental Celtic tribes and other Indo-European cultures. Known Celtic depictions of owls tend to be associated with votive cauldrons and other vessels, women's jewelry, and funerary statues, giving them a sense of connection with ritual contexts rather than being linked with war like other birds of prey. That many images of owls show them emerging out of, or being made up of, other beings as if they were depicted mid-metamorphosis, suggests a magical or Otherworldly correlation as well. Archaeologist Anne Ross believes the earliest owl images are Celtic devotional representations of an owl Goddess with origins in earlier European beliefs, potentially related to the figures of beaked Goddesses with round owl eyes dating back to the Neolithic period. This ancient Goddess was associated with both death and rebirth, a dual-aspect that both speaks to this divinity's liminality, as well as presages the positive and negative attitudes cultures held towards owls over time. (Ross 1996, 344)

Later Celtic Literature and Lore

In early Welsh literature, owls are consistently included in various listings of elder animals, a common international folk motif that features different animals depending upon the location of the story. The oldest Welsh iteration of this tale is found in *Culhwch and Olwen*; here, King Arthur and his men are on a quest to find Mabon, who was taken from his mother at three days old. They consult the five Oldest Animals of the Island of Britain in hopes that one of them would know the fate of Mabon. These are, from least to most ancient: the Blackbird of Cilgwri, the Stag of Redynfre, the Owl of Cwm Cowlyd, the Eagle of Gwern Abw, and the Salmon of Llyn Llyw.

When asked about Mabon, the Owl of Cwm Cowlyd replied:

"When first I came hither, the wide valley you see was a wooded glen. And a race of men came and rooted it up. And there grew there a second wood; and this wood is the third. My wings, are they not withered stumps? Yet all this time, even until today, I have never heard of the man for whom you inquire." (Guest, 124)

A similar listing can be found in Triad 92 of *Trioedd Ynys Prydein:*

The Three Elders of the World:
> The Owl of Cwm Cowlyd,
> the Eagle of Gwernabwy,
> and the Blackbird of Celli Gadarn.

Centuries later, a similar catalog, with the addition of the Toad o Cors, can be found in the Welsh folktale, "The Ancients of the World". In this story, the Eagle of Gwernabwy seeks the ancient pedigree of the Owl of Cwm Cowlyd to determine if she is old enough to be his wife; indeed, while Culhwch lists the Salmon as the Oldest of the Animals, this later tale accords that honor to the Owl. (Thomas, 148)

The significance of these Oldest Animals is uncertain. That they are consistently associated with particular places in Wales, some of which are difficult to locate with any surety, may point to totemistic animals associated with particular tribes or regions, which in turn may support the idea that the origins of the stories may pre-date Christianity in Britain. The stories themselves go out of their way to establish both the antiquity and longevity of these elder animals; this serves to place them outside of time - certainly beyond human memory - which gives them Otherworldly associations. It is notable that they are seen as allies; humans are shown consulting these ancient animals, who are willing to assist them.

As time progresses, however, there is a shift in the portrayal of owls in Celtic lore, likely in response to shifting religious beliefs as well as changes in the status of women, with whom owls are strongly associated. Similar to the conclusion of the Fourth Branch, several folktales from Wales and Brittany explain why the owl is hated by all other birds and fated to dwell in darkness; interestingly, these tales involve wrens and eagles - birds associated with Lleu.

In one Welsh tale, every bird gathered together to determine who among them would be their king. They decided that the bird who could fly the highest would receive that honor, and so they took to the sky, each flying as high as they could. At last, it was clear that the eagle was going to win this contest, but before he could claim his title, a tiny wren shot out from the now-tired eagle's feathers and flew even higher, winning the crown. Now, the rest of the birds were unhappy with the wren, and decided to drown the tiny bird in a pan of their tears - but before they could do so, the clumsy owl toppled over the pan and the wren was able to fly free. Unable to have their vengeance, the rest of the birds angrily attacked the owl and exiled her to live and hunt in the night. (Lawrence, 28)

A variant of the tale sees the birds pursue the wren for tricking the eagle. The tiny bird hides in a hedge, and none of the other birds can reach him. They take turns waiting for the wren to leave his hiding place, and the owl accidentally falls asleep on her watch, allowing the wren to escape. The owl is exiled for her failure. A Breton folktale tells how the wren tunneled down into the underworld to bring fire back up to the birds, burning its feathers off in the process. All of the birds donated one of their feathers to the wren in gratitude - all, save the owl, who was punished for her selfishness and made to hunt alone in the darkness. (Lawrence, 33)

These onomastic tales are accurate reflections of the behaviors of these birds; wrens do tend to make their nests low to the ground and in hedges, and other birds are known to mob and attack owls they come across during the day. Wrens are symbols of druidic magic, are considered the king of the birds, and are especially associated with the dying of the old year. This is further explored in Chapter 4.

Owls and the Dark Half

Owls were said to be the bird of Gwyn ap Nudd, the chthonic Welsh figure who was the leader of the Wild Hunt and Fairy King of Annwn; we have already discussed him as an example of the Otherworldly Champion in Chapter 4. In his poem "The Owl", early 14th century Welsh poet Dafydd ap Gwilym links the owl with Gwyn, while also alluding to Blodeuwedd in her owl form:

"Woe for her song (a wooden-collared roebuck),
And her face (features of a gentle woman),
And her shape; she's the phantom of the birds.
Every bird attacks her — she's dirty and she's exiled:
Is it not strange that she is alive?

Eloquently she used to howl — I know her face
She is a bird of Gwyn ap Nudd.
Garrulous owl that sings to thieves —
Bad luck to her tongue and tone!"

In Gaelic traditions, owls are connected with the Cailleach; a hag

Goddess and wise woman, her name literally translates as "veiled one", deriving from the Latin word "palladium". The tawny owl is called *Cailleach-oidhche* ("crone of the night") in Scots Gaelic, while the barn owl is *Cailleach-oidhche gheal* ("white old woman of the night") or *Cailleach-bhàn* ("white hag"). (Ross, 346).

The Cailleach is a powerful figure often seen as ruling over winter as its queen, and her name graces many landscape features throughout Ireland and Scotland. She has an ancestral aspect, much like the Owl in Culhwch and Olwen, and *The Yellow Book of Lecan* describes her has having been a young woman seven times, having married seven husbands, and having acted as foster mother to fifty children who went on to become the founders of many tribes and kingdoms. The Old Irish poem *Caillech Bérri* (*The Lament of the Old Woman of Beare*) which dates to the 8th century, seems to hint at her former status as a wanton lover of kings.

Many Cailleach traditions from Scotland, Ireland, and the Island of Man associate her with the changing of the seasons; sometimes she keeps a maiden captive to hold back the spring, and other times she herself has a youthful aspect during the Light Half of the Year. Taken together with her cycles of youth and old age, and traditions connecting her with particular places that bear her name, it is possible that the Cailleach was once a seasonal Sovereignty Goddess, and her owl represented the winter and the night.

Owls in Folklore and Practice

As nocturnal hunters, it is understandable that the owl would come to have associations with darker aspects of life, including death, misfortune, and illicit sexuality - especially of women. In Welsh folklore, hearing an owl call in a town or village is an announcement that an unmarried woman has lost her virginity; alternatively, if a woman hears the call of an owl while she is pregnant, it is a sign that her child has been blessed.

More often than not, however, hearing an owl's call presages death and destruction. In Welsh folk belief, the *aderyn y corph* - the corpse bird - is a horror to behold; it has no feathers or wings, yet flies mysteriously through the air. Its cry sounds like "Dewch! Dewch!" - the Welsh words for "Come! Come!" While the lore does not specify the kind of bird the aderyn y corph is supposed to be, the traditional Welsh name for the tawny owl is "aderyn corph", and the call of the female tawny owl is "'ke-wic", which sounds very similar to "dewch." (Sikes, 213)

A related belief is that hearing the shriek of a screech owl - which, in Britain, is a nickname for the barn owl due to the sounds it makes - outside of the window of an ill person indicates that they will soon die. The barn owl's call was also used to predict the weather - its shrieking heralded the coming of cold weather or the approach of a storm; however, hearing its call during bad weather meant that things were going to turn for the better.

Owl eggs and broth made from owls were believed to cure everything from whooping cough, to blindness, and gout. Eating the eggs raw was said to cure alcoholism and be protective for children. It was generally believed that witches could turn themselves into owls, and so owls could also be used to protect against witches and their magic. Nailing owls to barn doors were a protective measure against lightning and misfortune taken by farmers well into the 19th century. Today, they instead encourage owls to roost there by installing owl boxes, thus protecting their farms against vermin instead. It was believed that if you happened upon an owl in a tree, you could kill it by walking around the tree causing the bird to wring its own neck as it turned its head to follow you.

Blodeuwedd as Owl

There are five species of owl native to Britain: the tawny or brown owl (S*trix aluco*), the little owl (*Athene noctua*), the short-eared owl (*Asio flammeus*), the long-eared owl (*Asio otus*), and the barn owl (*Tyto alba*). The narrative of the Fourth Branch does not specify which species of owl Blodeuwedd is transformed into, saying only: "What Blodeuwedd is, is "owl" in the language of the present day... the owl is still called "flower-face" (*blodeuwedd*). (Ford, 108). There are medieval Welsh lexicons that attest to the use of the world "blodeuwedd" for owl, and the word is still in use by some modern Welsh speakers to refer to the species of bird in general, rather than any particular type of owl.

Kristoffer Hughes, head of the Anglesey Druid Order and native Welsh speaker, relayed the following to me: "In Caernarfonshire and Anglesey, the older folk would say, "*Nosweith dda Blodeuwedd*" ("Good evening, Blodeuwedd") at the hoot of an owl. It was a common phrase I'd hear as a child, so I still use it. I certainly don't think it's a diverse tradition, but probably an indication of the popularity of the tale in that region of Arfon where the Fourth Branch was mostly located."

For myself, even though there is no specific lore to support this, I have always seen Blodeuwedd as a barn owl. Their heart-shaped facial disks suggest her "flower-face" to me, and their ghostly white feathers spangled with brownish-red spots reminds me of the white and red animals associated with the Otherworld in Celtic mythos.

I was curious to know which owl others have come to associate with her, and so - without disclosing my own experience - I used social media to conduct an informal survey of Pagans and polytheists who feel a connection to, or are actively engaged in a devotional relationship with, Blodeuwedd. I received 63 replies, and some people included their stories and experiences: 31 people associated her with barn owls, 11 with snowy owls, 8 with great horned owls, 3 with tawny owls, 3 with any owl, 2 with barred owls, and 1 each for gray, bard, and eagle owls. I find it interesting that so many people shared my Unverified Personal Gnosis (UPG) on this, although a quick survey of Blodeuwedd art overwhelmingly associates her with barn owls as well, which speaks to the artists' UPG as well as the potential unconscious influence their art may have had on others. However, there is something to be said for her coming to each of us in a guise that was often reflective of the places we lived and the experiences we have had with owls in our lives.

In Blodeuwedd, we see a culmination of many owl beliefs and attributes. Some of them appear to have a more ancient origin, referencing the shape-changing qualities of the owl which harken back to their earliest artifactual representations. Her role as a seasonal Sovereignty Goddess can be seen as a reflection of the female owl divinity posited by Anne Ross, particularly concerning her dual nature in ruling over fertility and death. And finally, Blodeuwedd's infidelity is reflective of the medieval association of owls with illicit sexuality - a meaning underscored by separate folkloric traditions which see women transformed into owls as punishment for their sexual transgressions.

Chapter 7

Seeking Sovereignty

Reclaiming Blodeuwedd's identity as a Sovereignty Goddess is a powerful experience of mind and heart, requiring both study and devotion. Whether or not she was worshiped as a divinity in ancient times, she holds deep resonance as the Sovereign Lady of the Seasons, whose embrace empowers the Lord of the Summer and the Lord of the Winter in turn, and there is no question that she is honored by many modern pagans and polytheists as a Goddess today.

I believe it to be significant that this reclamation and revisioning of Blodeuwedd's story is happening in the here and now. I see mythology as a reflection of the collective needs of the culture which birthed it, and when tales and folklore remain in orality - as with Celtic British tradition - they are able to evolve to reflect the changing needs of that culture.

So why are the stories of the Welsh Gods increasingly being retold, especially in the last few decades? Why have these Gods been awakened and taking root in our collective consciousness - not just in Wales (where the stories have remained alive as part of their cultural fabric, albeit not in a religious context) but all over the world? What lessons do these Gods hold for us as modern seekers and practitioners? Why are they making themselves known in the world again, and how can we be in service to them through our work and devotion?

For no matter where we may live, our present-day culture and its symbol-sets are quite different from what they were when these stories were written down. Our leaders are not tested or chosen by a representative of the land they seek to rule, and our science has demonstrated the process by which our world experiences the seasonal round. What significance, then, does a

Sovereignty Goddess hold for us in the modern world? In this era when individuality is prized over collectivity, and general disconnection from the rhythms of Earth, and moon, and sun is the norm in the Western world, perhaps we are not meant to begin our journey of relationship with Sovereignty by seeking her in the world around us. Perhaps we must start by finding her in the world within us. Perhaps we are being called to establish a sovereignty of the self, which will empower us to honor the sovereignty of others as we work cooperatively towards restoring a much-needed balance between humanity and our world.

When we reflect these tales within, we can come to an understanding of Sovereignty as it applies to the self. I have come to define Sovereignty to mean "fully conscious self-determination". This can be achieved by working towards the wholeness that comes when we endeavor to bring the unconscious self into consciousness, a process of self-knowledge that catalyzes inner change and personal growth. We can reclaim the mythic process outlined in Blodeuwedd's story as a guiding practice for coming into our personal sovereignty, as it assists us in discovering our True Will and shows how to live a life that is a reflection of our hard-won knowledge of our authentic self.

In order to become Sovereign, we must first understand the inner culture that has arisen within us in response to the topography and climate of our personal landscape. This landscape is comprised of our mental, emotional, and physical bodies; these have been shaped by our experiences and reflect the current degree of balance that exists within and between each of these aspects of the self.

In my experience and belief, the reclamation of our sovereignty over these inner landscapes is the work that Blodeuwedd is calling us to do.

Following the Mythic Map

Blodeuwedd acts as the point around which the seasons turn from one to the other - from the fertile, fragrant abundance of the Light Half of the Year to the decaying, chthonic stillness of the Dark Half the Year. She is the doorway between states of being, and it is our work to find that fulcrum of balance within ourselves as well. As a mirror of the work we have done to restore Blodeuwedd's essence as a Sovereignty figure - both in our academic understanding of her, and as a devotee coming into relationship with her - it can be helpful for us to emulate the journey she undertakes in her story.

Just as we worked to reclaim her stature as a Sovereignty Goddess - recasting the meaning of her tale and the purpose of her journey - so must we seek to recenter ourselves in our authentic purpose... always striving to walk the path of our lives as a reflection of our Sovereignty - as Blodeuwedd teaches - no matter what the cost. But how can we know where that path lies? What is the nature of our Sovereignty?

One way to engage in this self-reflective process is to apply to our own lives the same criteria we used to determine Blodeuwedd's status as a Sovereignty Goddess in Chapter 3. It is a powerful exercise to ask ourselves these questions, meditate upon their answers, and use the resulting insights to guide us along the next step of our life's journey. This process of seeing her story within our own story is a devotional act that can clarify and strengthen our relationship with Blodeuwedd. Then, as we progress in relationship with her, we can seek her guidance as we work through our challenges. How privileged we are to have such a powerful ally at our side as we undertake this work!

Self-Reflective Questions for our Inner Sovereignty

1. *Sovereignty and the Land.* What is the nature of your inner landscape? How well do you know the details and contours of your domain, that is to say, your personal

91

make-up: what are your gifts and your challenges, what are your triumphs and your fears? What facets of yourself are still in need of exploration? What resources are at your disposal, and how well do you manage them? Over what aspects of your life do you already claim Sovereignty? To whom - or in service to what - have you given parts of your power away? Where do you most need to reclaim your sovereignty?

2. *Sovereignty and Liminality.* What is the state of your personal boundaries, on every level of existence: physical, mental, emotional, and spiritual? Where are these boundaries in need of strengthening, and where might they benefit from being a bit thinned? How well do you know the extent of your domain, and what do you do to maintain it? How well do you honor the boundaries of others? Where does your influence begin and end in every aspect of your life, including your inner and outer environments, your relationships, and your engagement with the world?

3. *Sovereignty and the Hunt.* How clear are you about your life's work? What goals have you set for yourself? What dreams are you actively pursuing? What are you willing to do to manifest the truth of your Sovereign self? What are you currently struggling with in pursuit of the reclamation of your personal power? What past lessons can you draw upon to help you with your present challenges? What past experiences must you come to peace with or leave behind so that you can move forward?

4. *Sovereignty as Tester of Potential Kings.* Can you discern a pattern of challenges in your life which seem to be presenting themselves to you over and over again? Why do you think this might be? What has your response to

these challenges been in the past, and what might you do differently in the present or the next time they come around? In what ways can you reframe these challenges so that you can view them as opportunities for growth and change, rather than punishments for lessons unlearned?

5. *Sovereignty and the Sacred Marriage.* In what areas of your life have you been able to attain a sense of balance? Where are the places of imbalance and what needs to be done to address them? Where does the balance of power lie in the context of the relationships in your life - with your partner, members of your family, in your work environment, in your community, with the Divine, and with yourself? How clearly can you hear the voice of your intuitive self? How much trust and discernment have you developed when it comes to consciously seeking out the wisdom that lies within?

6. *The Withdrawal of Sovereignty.* Over what areas of your life do you not presently wield agency? Where have you had to withdraw your energies, and why? Are there parts of your inner landscape that have been overtaken by the Wasteland - places which no longer grow, gifts and abilities no longer used, resources no longer available, energies completely depleted? Why do you think this is? How can you restore Sovereignty over these areas? How can you reallocate your energies in order to bring these places back to life? Where do you need to release your expectations, acknowledge the impact and truth of your limitations, and allow yourself to put down the burden of situations which can only be accepted but never changed?

7. *Sovereignty as Shape Changer.* What does your life look like in the present moment? How do you view your present

circumstance and your place within it? How positive or negative is your self-concept? How does the person you seek to be differ from the person you currently are? As you reclaim more and more of your personal Sovereignty, how does this shift the way your life looks? How does this shift how you see yourself? What must be done to affect these changes? What is the nature of the bridge you need to build in order to move yourself from where you are to where you seek to be? What does it look like when your life, or parts of your life, are in a place of imbalance? How can you learn to recognize the signs of this imbalance so that you can act to bring yourself back to a place of balance sooner?

Embracing our Darkness

Just as Blodeuwedd partnered with Gronw, just as the Otherworldly Champion is favored for a time by the Lady of Sovereignty, just as the Earth beds down for a while enfolded by winter, the reclamation of our Sovereignty requires that we actively enter the Shadow within us, and embrace the challenges that arise in our lives. We must be willing to spread our owl wings and hunt for the seeds of our authenticity which have been relegated to the shrouded corners of our deepest selves - hiding there, away from the criticism, disapproval, and socially reinforced belief of their impossibility or lack of worth.

We must seek these seeds with owl sight and hold them tightly with sharpened talons. To find true Sovereignty, we must spend time in the darkness and come to know every valley and contour of our inner lands - both where it is abundant and where it is fallow. Then, we must learn how to honor and bless these parts of ourselves. We must cultivate a practice of self-compassion, even as we actively engage in our own healing, rather than engage in the toxic spiritual bypassing that denies any aspect of our inner darkness - a flawed paradigm which ultimately only serves to keep the truth of who we are imprisoned in the places we pretend not to see.

Wholeness is achieved when we are able to acknowledge and accept all aspects of ourselves even as we strive to become the best self we can be. It is only by acknowledging where our inner landscape is fallow that we can know what work is necessary to bring this manifestation of the Wasteland back to life. We are beings of light and darkness, and the call of Blodeuwedd is to find our way to the place where all of the seeming contradictions of our total selves are resolved. In Jungian terms, the integration of Shadow leads us to the transcendence of individuation - the authenticity of personal Sovereignty.

And like the seasons of the year, the phases of moon, and the circuit of the day which sees us pass from darkness to light and back again, we must learn how to surrender ourselves to the turning of Cycle, and to harness the wisdom of its process as it moves both around us and through us. We need not fear the dark or struggle against it, nor should we shun the light or avoid the vulnerability of its illumination. Like Blodeuwedd, we have different tools at our disposal during each season, and each season brings us different work to do.

Celebrating the Flower Maiden

Reclaiming Blodeuwedd as a Sovereignty Goddess requires that we reclaim and resanctify the totality of who she is - to seek and find the divinity in both Blodeuedd and Blodeuwedd. This is no small thing. It is easy to see Blodeuwedd in her owl form as possessing personal power: she is wisdom embodied, keen-sighted and laser-focused on what she wants, able to fly where she wills of her own volition - a solitary figure who is powerful, silent, and unafraid, even in the darkest of night.

But what of Blodeuedd, the Flower Maiden? It is easy to dismiss this version of her as a hollow artifice - the illusion that stands in stark contrast to the power of her owl form. After all, what more could she be but a symbol of patriarchy's ideal woman? Someone created to meet a man's need and to fulfill the purpose delegated to her - no more and no less. She is an object that is constructed out of insubstantial stuff; how could she do anything but reflect the most superficial and transient attributes of the fragile blooms from which she was wrought?

For flowers, by their very nature, are not meant to last. They are beautiful, intoxicating, and impermanent. In much of literature, the sought-after maiden is praised for her beauty, prized for her innocence, and pursued for her youth. Like the easily-bruised petals of a flower, she is fragile and in need of protection. She has her season, and her worth is in her function; the fertilized flower becomes the fruit, and a woman's best destiny - according to the patriarchy - is to be a mother.

And so Blodeuedd begins her tale as the perfect wife - beautiful, compliant, and silent. She is accepting of her place and fully participates in her given role - and why would she do otherwise? She doesn't know that there are other options, or that there are any other ways of being - until she falls in love. It is love which sets her soul aflame. Love which enlivens her being. Love which causes her to recognize for the first time that her life is her own, and that she has the power to choose her own course and to set her own trajectory.

Perhaps it is this acknowledgement of her individuality and the sacred nature of personal will which caused her to transcend her form - to become a soul enshrouded in a body - to be filled with the spark of true life, and to experience the first kindling of wisdom. Indeed, her sense of individuality comes through as we hear her speak for the first time in the narrative. Once she has realized her own agency, Blodeuedd begins to act in support of her own desires. She has thrown off her programming, and what she says and does is now deemed worthy of note in the tale, precisely because it stands in contrast to expectation.

Now that she knows what she wants and learns what she

needs to do to obtain it, she discovers that the source of her power comes from the very things that were intended to make her feel weak. Like the heady scent of flowers, her beauty is disarming. Her petal-like fragility engenders the impulse in others to protect her, and her newly-budded innocence has her present as being incapable of guile.

And so, she is underestimated by those around her - and this allows her to use the attributes built into her by her creators in a way they could never have imagined. For the oak grows strong and tall, and permits far-seeing. Tenacious broom grips the earth tightly and sweeps away all obstacles. Fragrant meadowsweet dulls the senses and assists in the crossing of boundaries - and through carried by the bride, it also accompanies the dead into their graves.

Oak, broom, and meadowsweet. These are the components of her being. These are the gifts she was given by her creators. These are the tools at her disposal. We do Blodeuedd a great disservice by calling her a manipulator when, in truth, she was making use of the resources available to her. And once she was able to use them to achieve her ends and create a life she loved, she changed and grew and obtained deep wisdom.

Flowers to Feathers

Our own path to growth and Sovereign wholeness is a mirror of the Flower Maiden's journey, and we will do well to respect and honor her. For each of us, no matter our gender, are a reflection of the patriarchal culture that has formed us from the moment of our birth. Like tender plants, we are cultivated to fulfill a purpose, and to yield a specific harvest; when we seek to grow in ways which fall outside of these expectations, we meet the pruner's shears, while rich fertilizer is provided where we remain in alignment with the roles placed upon us. The windows are transparent in the greenhouse of the over-culture, letting us see enough of the wild outdoors to believe that we are growing there - but the truth is that the structure will not permit us to take root in those fertile soils.

Unless we choose change. Unless we take action to break free of the confines placed upon us and live a life of our own making. And how can we do this?

Like Blodeuedd, we must learn to recognize the spark of desire in our hearts and allow this passion to grow within us, empowering us to use this creative energy to manifest a life that we love. Just as flowers turn their faces to follow the track of the sun, when the spark of desire builds to become the fire of True Will within us, we will birth forth an inner sun - catalyzing a new and more authentic trajectory for our lives.

When we do not follow the same source of light as the rest of society, when we make changes in accordance with our inner passions rather than those we are programmed to have by the over-culture, we will seem strange to them... branded as Other. When we leave the greenhouse of enculturation, we become boundary dwellers, living in ways and in places that do not make sense to the glass-encased world of ordered rows and regulated temperatures. When our source of light comes from within, we are able to see clearly in the darkness. We recognize illusion for what it is, and have obtained the skills necessary to obtain our goals and hold tight to our truths, no matter what hatred and scorn may come our way.

But before we learn to see with owl sight or grow our wings to fly where we will, we must first acknowledge and honor the truth of our flower-formed self - that frame which we have been cultivated to wear since the moment of our birth - and to find the power embodied there, even if we believe it to be our weakness. To do so, we must identify - without judgement, without the poison of self-recrimination - the components that have been brought together to create us: the circumstances of our lives, the skills we have developed, the tools we have obtained, and the experiences we have lived through.

To begin this process, we can meditate upon our own flower form and the three things necessary for a flower to grow: soil, water, and sunlight. It can be helpful to seek out the answers to these questions in order to get a sense of who we are in the here and the now:

1. *Soil* - What is the nature of the soil where we plant our roots? Where is our home, our foundation, the facts of our environment? What social structures and relationship dynamics are at play in our lives? How strong are our boundaries? How safe do we feel? What is the availability of necessary resources? Where are we stuck or unmoving? What limitations or illusions have we accepted? What are our strengths? Where is the center of our power? What skills do we possess? What tools are at our disposal?

2. *Water* - Where do we obtain the water we need to live? Are our emotional needs being met, and our ability to express them unhindered? Are these waters plentiful, or are they apportioned conditionally? Are these waters pure and clear, or do they carry with them the residue of toxicity or the taint of expectation? What is the nature of our relationship with ourselves? With others? With the Divine? How do we practice compassion and seek understanding, both for ourselves and others?

3. *Sunlight* - What is the source of our life's light? What feeds us and gives us direction? What brings us joy and fulfillment? What moves us away from suffering? What motivates our actions? What guides our choices? What are our life's goals? When and why did we set them? What is our relationship with our Shadow?

Implicitly or otherwise, we are cultivated to conform to the expectations of others and to use our gifts in service to the roles placed upon us. Once we are conscious of who we are, what are we made of, and how we came to be where we are in the here and now, then we can assess how closely aligned our lives are with the even the smallest spark of True Will that resides within us - how much we resemble the vision of the Sovereign self that we hold in our deepest and most authentic heart.

Chapter 8

Entering into Relationship with Blodeuwedd

It is possible to foster a strong and authentic relationship with Blodeuwedd; as with any divinity, the key, in my opinion, is to build a bridge between the self and the divine. As with the construction of any bridge you will need a blueprint, the proper tools, resources in the form of building materials, and energy expended through time and work to manifest your will. For this inner bridge to take form, the blueprint is revealed through study, the tools are developed through practice, and the resources are gathered and expended through devotion.

Study - Hopefully, the information presented in this book has provided a solid foundation from which to begin or deepen a study of Blodeuwedd through immersion into her story, an exploration of its meaning when examined through a medieval Welsh cultural context, and the lessons this divine lady holds for us today.

Practice - There is no one way to approach creating a practice around making a connection to Blodeuwedd. What follows is an offering intended both to provide some concrete guidance on how to begin building a practice, and to serve as a jumping off point for the creation of our own practices, inspired by the insights you've received from Blodeuwedd herself.

Devotion - We can look at devotion as both the energy expended while weaving together the threads of insights gathered through the acts of study and practice, as well as the beautiful tapestry that results from our striving, representing the true and lived experience of our connection to Source. Devotion is both what we do and what we create; it is the heart-centered intention to come into relationship - without ego, expectation, or fear. It is the art of dedicating some time, energy, and space toward the goal of fostering relationship without agenda or expectation.

Celtic Religious Practices

Aside from the accounts of Classical writers, which mostly focused on the practices of the Druids in their sacred groves, we do not have any written record about how Celtic Pagans interacted with their Gods. The archaeological record, however, provides us with some indirect information about Celtic beliefs. They propitiated the Gods with votive offerings, often by ritually breaking and depositing high status items in bodies of water. They practiced human sacrifice, likely when things were particularly dire, although we do not know how willing the victims may have been. They buried their dead with items which appear to reflect their work or station in life, apparently including them to ensure that they had access to these things in the next life. They venerated their ancestors, making offerings to them especially at times and in places of liminality. When they started to create images of their Gods after the influence of Rome, they appear to have erected personal shrines in their homes as indicated by the presence of small devotional statuary.

When Rome took over Celtic lands and began to syncretize native divinities with their own, we begin to see dedicatory stele and altars erected to Romano-Celtic Gods. In the face of this material culture, we have been able to determine that some divinities are local and connected to the land, while others have more far-ranging worship.

At places like the Temple of Sulis-Minerva at Bath, we see the Romano-British practice of curse tablets cast into the waters of the sacred spring; these lead tablets - which ask for the intervention of the Goddess to punish those who have stolen from or otherwise wronged the petitioner - include both Roman and British names. In those same waters, we have also found votive offerings to Sulis-Minerva that were crafted to resemble body parts; these are believed to either represent what the petitioner has asked the Goddess to heal, or were given in thanks for a healing already received.

As we have already discussed, by the time the stories - which we believe may have origins in Pagan times - were written down, the Welsh had been solidly Christian for almost eight centuries. Something that stands out in the legendarium of Wales is the unquestioned proximity of the Otherworld; it is not unusual for someone to slip into the Otherworld, or for Otherworldly beings to cross over into this world. If we consider the Otherworld and its inhabitants to be the mythic remnants of divinities and spirits of place venerated in Pagan times, perhaps this tells us something important about the way the typical ancient Briton saw themselves and their world in relation to the Gods.

If that is the case, then the Gods were everywhere, dwelling in the landscape, and particularly accessible through places and times of liminality. Their favor and assistance could be obtained or acknowledged through the giving of offerings, and their protection could be secured through sacrifice and the use of ritual items, such as the burial of horse skulls in the thresholds of houses. Certain folk practices observed in the past 200 years, such as the winter mumming party of the Mari Lwyd and the Hunting of the Wren on St. Stephen's day, may be remnants of ancient beliefs, although they may simply be a reflection of an ongoing relationship between humans and the land they live on, regardless of religious origins.

With these things in mind, we can craft a practice of devotion to Blodeuwedd which emulates aspects of what we do know about Celtic practice and belief; these in turn can be used to assist in fostering a connection that builds a relationship with her. The gifting of offerings on a shrine or altar; the pouring of libations at places of liminality like river banks or lake-sides, or boundary places like gates or bridges; the performing of rituals at threshold times, like sunset or at the first quarter moon - these are helpful clues which can inform our practice. However, bigger than this, we see that there is a pattern of individual connection with the divine. The proximity of the Otherworld in myth may indicate how very accessible these forces were; no formal priesthood was required to mediate every experience, although conventions of hospitality and respect were necessary for these connections to be successful and positive.

What follows, therefore, are some suggestions to help with fostering a personal relationship with Blodeuwedd. In addition to studying her story and identifying the symbolism in her tale that reflects her core nature and the lessons she holds for us, creating a devotional shrine is a good place to start forging a connection with her. I have also included a journey to help to connect with her in her guises of Flower Maiden and Owl, which will assist in experiencing her different energies and allow us to actively seek her guidance in how we can reclaim Sovereignty in our own lives.

Devotional Work

The creation of an altar (a working space for ritual or magic) or shrine (a devotional space for honoring divinity and fostering daily mindfulness) dedicated to Blodeuwedd is a powerful statement of a desire to enter into a relationship with her. Guided by the Hermetic Principle of Correspondence which says that like energies attract each other, the study of Blodeuwedd's story can inform the choice of objects to place upon her shrine. Here are some ideas to get started:

- *Images of Blodeuwedd* - all manner of art and statuary depicting Blodeuwedd are available for purchase; of course, it is a powerful act of devotion to create the image oneself.

- *Images of owls and owl feathers* - Statuary, art prints, and feathers are wonderful ways to tie into the energies of Owl. Be sure that the possession of owl feathers is legal before obtaining them, as this is not the case everywhere. Using feathers from other birds with similar coloring and markings can serve as symbolic alternatives.

- *Flowers of oak, broom, and meadowsweet* - These blooms can be collected and placed on the altar as an offering, or burnt as an incense to honor her. Similarly, images of these flowers or flower essences made from these blooms can help create a bridge between the seeker and the Goddess.

- *Images of sites associated with Blodeuwedd* - Photographs or paintings of Tomen y Mur and Llyn Morwynion, stones charged in these places, and water taken from the lake itself are wonderful connections to her mythic landscape. My shrine includes a small replica of Llech Ronw that I fashioned out of clay; I have visited this standing stone many times on pilgrimage, and the hole speaks to me of the portal between the worlds that Blodeuwedd embodies.

Of Flowers and Feathers - A Journey

Set aside a place and time where you will not be disturbed. Sit in front of your shrine or working altar dedicated to Blodeuwedd. Read through the working beforehand so you are prepared for the journey. Consider memorizing or mapping out the key points of the journey, or recording it as a guide so that you can be as present as possible for the journey as it unfolds. Consider writing out the invocations for Blodeuedd and Blodeuwedd on an index card that you keep on your altar, so that you have it on hand for when you need it. Be sure to have your journal close by so that you can record your experiences and insights at the end of the working.

Close your eyes and establish an even and rhythmic breath. Once this pattern becomes natural, focus upon this breath. As you exhale, release any energies that prevent you from being fully present in body, mind, and spirit. As you inhale, envision vibrant green energies of Earth being pulled up through your root and filling the entirety of your energy field with its vitalistic energies. Continue to cycle your breath in this way until you feel centered, clear, and open. When you are ready, begin the journey.

Envision yourself standing on a cliffside overlooking a lake. The sky blushes as it births the dawn, and the steadily rising sun paints the world around you with a wash of pale color.

Feel yourself warmed by the growing light as it illuminates the landscape.

Touching you with its gilded rays, the sunshine transforms into a vortex of yellow and white flowers that swirl and dance around you.

Delicate threads of oak blossoms weave a silken garment around you, and as it enrobes your form, feel yourself grow strong in body, limitless in energy, and youthful in spirit.

Yellow petals of broom gather around your head, converging to cover it like a golden veil. As it descends, feel your mind clear, your thoughts broaden, and your vision expand.

A rain of white meadowsweet envelops your senses, intoxicating you with their honeyed, heady scent. Any physical and emotional discomfort disappears as you feel yourself uplifted by a sense of profound peace and radiating bliss.

Take three, deep, centering breaths. Immerse yourself in this moment, high above the upland valley lake, bathed in sunlight, surrounded by the flowers of oak, broom, and meadowsweet.

Fully in the moment, you become keenly aware of the movement of the sun as it arcs along its path, brightening the sky. Turn towards the sun. Savor its warmth on your face. Feel a spark kindle to life in your chest. Envision a bridge taking form between this small inner flame and the vast celestial sun. Feel the connection between them grow stronger as the sun climbs higher, until you experience the two become one.

Allow this inner flame to fill your heart. Ask that the light of its truth illuminate the Sovereign pathway within, revealing the bountiful harvest of your gifts as well as the seeds of potential laying dormant within you. Feel the vitalistic power of the sun nurture what is already growing, and activate what has been patiently awaiting the light of your awareness.

Breathe into these places. Feel your heart open to all possibilities, as the flowers of your potential unfold, drinking in the light.

When you are ready, call to Blodeuedd, Lady of Flowers, to guide you, saying these words or those of your own choosing:

Blodeuedd, Flower Bride
Lady of meadowsweet, oak flowers, and broom:
Lend me your vision to track the light's pathways
Show me the way-signs to guide my life's journey
Teach me to open and embrace my soul's potential
With fragrant and fertile ecstasy
Through the fields of my authenticity

In this moment, know that the soft touch of the blossoms around you is her touch; your fragrance, hers - your radiance, hers. Feel for her presence, and take three deep, centering breaths to connect as fully with her energy as you can.

When you are ready, ask Blodeuedd to show you a vision of yourself - fully actualized and centered in authenticity. Take what time you need to see this image of your Sovereign self with clarity.

When you are ready, ask what you need most to know at this point in your life's journey to acknowledge and support the manifestation of your sacred purpose. What is your next step along the path to embrace your Sovereignty?

Spend some time journeying with Blodeuedd, seeking these answers, and being open to these experiences and all of the ways that information can come to you: symbols, visions, voices, emotions, memories, and just a general sense of knowing. Do not judge, just receive.

When you feel you have completed this part of the journey, thank Blodeuedd for her guidance. When you are ready, bring your attention back to the hillside where you stand in the now-waning light.

The sun disappears below the western horizon. The sky is dark and shimmers with stars. A cold wind rushes towards you and disperses the petals that surround you, scattering them into the deepening night.

Shivering, you wrap your arms around your shoulders and notice that your skin has become blanketed by a soft downy coat. A strange prickling sensation overtakes you as long white plumes emerge from your flesh, replacing the down. Soon you are completely enrobed, as if wearing a cloak of feathers.

You continue to transform as the moon climbs higher in the sky. Your feet become talons. Your arms are now fully-fledged wings. Your body becomes smaller and lighter, and a tail fans out behind you.

Your face widens and flattens into a heart-shaped disc of feathers that collect even the smallest of sounds, sending them to your now-asymmetrical ears. The merest whisper of a rustling in the distance behind you catches your attention. Turning towards it, you realize you now have the ability to rotate your head almost completely around you. A screech of surprise arises from your throat, passing through your sharp yellow beak.

Your eyes grow larger and many times sharper, allowing you to see the surrounding landscape with a clarity that mimics daylight.

Breathe into this new body, this owl form you now embody. Feel the strength of your talons, the freedom of your wings, the clarity of your hearing, and the truth of your sight.

Experience how these changes have empowered you with tools and abilities to meet the challenges that come with the night.

When you are ready, call to Blodeuwedd, Owl Goddess, to guide you, saying these words or those of your own choosing:

Blodeuwedd, Flower Faced One
Hunter through nights dark and moons bright
Lend me your vision to see through the shadow
Show me the truth that lays beyond all illusion
Teach me to grasp my Sovereignty with iron-gripped talons
And to fly on silent, unerring wings
Through the skies of my destiny

In this moment, know the softness of the feathers around you are her feathers; your wings are hers, your talons - hers. Feel for her presence, and take three deep, centering breaths to connect as fully with her energy as you can.

When you are ready, ask Blodeuwedd to reveal the aspects of yourself that prevent you from fully embodying your Sovereignty. Take what time you need to see this vision of your Shadow self with clarity.

When you are ready, ask Blodeuwedd what you need most to know at this point in your life's journey that will help you overcome your fears, and release your outmoded beliefs about who you are and what you are capable of becoming. Ask her to show you what tools you have at your disposal that will help you reclaim the truth of who you are.

Spend some time journeying with Blodeuwedd, seeking these answers, and being open to the experiences and all of the ways that information can come to you: symbols, visions, voices, emotions, memories, and just a general sense of knowing. Do not judge, just receive.

When you feel you have completed this part of the journey, thank Blodeuwedd for her guidance. When you are ready, bring your attention back to the hillside where you stand in the deep, still darkness of the night.

Take a moment to integrate and remember all that you have seen and experienced, with three deep, centering breaths.

A single bird sings out, greeting the barest hint of dawn. A warm breeze from the east envelops you, loosening your feathers and carrying them away into the darkness.

Find yourself in your own form once more, standing on the hilltop where this journey began.

In your hands, envision a bowl full of the sweetest honey wine. Fill it with the energies of gratitude for all that you have received, and when you are ready - as you stand there at the threshold of dawn - pour it out as a libation to honor the Sovereign Lady who has been such a gracious guide for this journey. Speak what words of thanks arise from the bottom of your heart.

Take three more breaths. Open your eyes, and return to waking consciousness.

With your breath and intention, ground and center - releasing any excess energies you may have brought back with you - until you feel yourself in a place of energetic balance.

The journey is complete.

Be sure to journal your insights and experiences.

Chapter 9

Forward into the Future

Unseasonably chilly, even for Wales in the summer, we walked through the patches of mist clinging damply to the undulating Snowdonia landscape. I had been here several times before, and I've seen this landscape wearing many different seasonal garments. But this time, there was something different.

Certainly, I was not the same person who had last set her pilgrim's feet upon this cobbled stretch of Roman road, part of the ancient trackways called Sarn Elen. Only sheep and the occasional hikers now walk this path, winding past the ruins of a Roman amphitheater and an 18th century farmhouse, leading to the dual-humped remains of the Norman motte-and-bailey castle Tomen y Mur ("The Mound of the Wall"), built on the site of a Roman fort. In the Fourth Branch, it is called Mur Castell, and was Lleu and Blodeuwedd's chief court.

This was her land, and it was she we had come to meet. The ruins before me are as layered as her tale, and what can presently be seen in the landscape only hints at the complexity of what lies beneath, built upon a foundation of an even more distant past. Neolithic and Roman, Celtic and Norman, 18th century and today.

Down in the valley below us is the decommissioned Trawsfynydd Nuclear Power Station - a stark intruder in this otherwise timeless pastoral scene. I am conscious that each step takes me further away from the encompassing present and deeper into the nebulous energies of the past. Away from the power of science, and deeper into the power of myth...of story and of symbol expressing itself through the very land around us.

This is the land of the Flower Bride, the woman made of flowers so that she could be wed to the Scion of Gwynedd, in defiance - or fulfillment - of his mother's wishes. I have sought her here before when the land was awash with flowers - purple rosebay willowherb, yellow gorse, white meadowsweet. But this time, it was different. This time, I went not to the mound but wandered instead along the grass-enrobed earthworks near the ruins of stone walls, lingering a bit to listen as I stood between the berried hawthorn trees.

This time, I saw instead the tall-tufted wild onion growing between the stones of the invader's roads. I saw enormous patches of nettle, sheltering against the broken masonry of the Norman encampment. I saw purple thistle, squatting and hardy against the winds racing up from the valley, from the power plant and beyond.

And yet, this was she. Expressing herself, leaving her Sovereign imprint across this land. A force of nature responding to the needs of this place in this time. Seeking to bring things into a balanced relationship, offering what is most needed.

She is a shape-shifter. Becoming what she must. Reclaiming the ruins that criss-cross her landscape, half-healed scars that nonetheless hold the stories of the past... just as our own scars hold the memory of who we have been, providing us with a map that charts our journey to the present.

She is awake. She is alive. She is more than what her tale portrays her to be. Much more. The ancestral spirits of this land rejoice, for she was never meant to be frozen in time, nor constrained by any boundaries - be they stone walls or a static story. Not oak, broom, and meadowsweet now, no... new medicine is required today. She reveals herself to me as a potent decoction of nettle and thistle and wild onion. Where once she was a bridal bouquet of pleasure and beauty, she now pierces the flesh with her tiny spines, burns the skin with her acrid sting, and slices the air with her pungent odor. My wet cheeks bear witness to her threefold power to make me cry.

Standing there amid the wild growth tumbling over the

reclaimed ruins of what has been, I ask her what she has to say to those who seek her today... those who wish to emulate her tale, to follow in her rebellion, to risk everything for the chance to live the life they long for... What guidance can she share with those who wish to walk a path of Sovereignty?

And this Onion Maiden - Goddess, guardian - with strands of stinging nettle blooms for her hair, and the protective spines of thistles covering her flesh, gifted me with this poem, and I am honored to share it now with you.

Thistle, and nettle, and wild onions
Grow between crumbling walls and ancient ruins
Windswept upon the hilltop.

Books are for pressing flowers between their pages
While castles are for oppressing Flower Maidens
Taken from their wild places -
Forced to speak a language of sound,
To sing another's song...
To trade green blood for red.

You can plant flowers in rows...
but not so women,
or owls.
Like seeds, they fly where they will -
taking root where they find purchase
to bloom another day.

Onions and nettles and thistles:
This is her new recipe.
Why did Gwydion not gather these?
Why did he not conjure life into these?
Perhaps because of the tears they each bring
and, having suffered enough,

he thought Lleu would do best to avoid them.

But the land knows what is needed
For healing
For wholeness.
And acrid though the remedies may be,
It is necessary that we know life's sting,
taste life's bitterness,
have our blood drawn by life's thorny fingers -
to honor the Queen, to call to her Sovereignty.

She lives here still, though her flowers are different.
She dwells here yet, enlivening the land with her talon-sharp
    fragrance.
The touch of her fingers spread fire:
you will not soon forget the heat of her caress on your flesh.

Pungent and sharp-spired, she lingers.
Grasping the hem of our garments,
She bids us:

Take me with you!
Know the truth of this life.
Let your strength be increased by it
Even as your tears flow as you cut me!
Consume me!
Boil me as pottage!
My nettle is stinging medicine.
My onion, sharp sister to every food.
My thistle, reminders of what has been...
what has gone
and what will come again.
For I am still here. Still Sovereign.
I mark these lands as my own.

I no longer require a sacrificial king;
Your thistle-drawn blood is all the offering I need.

Know my truth:
Some flowers are sweet salves, and some deadly poisons
and NONE may be kept in captivity for long -
Not by men
Or magicians
Or gods
Or old stories.
I am free in this landscape:
windblown and wild.
AND NONE MAY TAME ME AGAIN.

Write me a new song to be carried
by nine bells across the sea:
Nine waves of rages
Of righteous women's anger
Of boundaries defended
Of NEVER AGAIN

Stand fast and claim what they tried and failed to take:
the right to your voice
to fill your form completely
to love freely
to change your mind
to transform your life
and never give up the power wrest
from the hands of Gwydion
and those like him
by those who have paid the price in full.

Be owls, my sisters!
Be wise, and unerring in your aim,

your moon-ensilvered sight clear of illusion.
But also be flowers,
and plant your own gardens.
Follow your own pathway.
Walk the golden trackway beneath
the conqueror's stones:
the ancient road, Sarn Elen -
so that you may bloom
so that you may become
all that you are meant to be.

Oh! What can you expect from me when you visit out of
    season?
What but nettles, and thistles, and wild onion?
The hawthorn, too... with only memories of May bloomings
instead, bearing berries
scaled with silver lichens
draped messily with fairy wool.

But take these offerings, these gifts, these wisdoms.
Weave for me a new crown
A true crown.

I am no longer what I was.
I am not yet what I shall be.
But you must know me, here and now,
If you wish to know my truth and taste my mystery
If you wish for my tale to continue
If you wish to carry me home.

JT 8/19
Tomen y Mur

And so, as it should be, her story continues...

Bibliography

Primary Sources

C. Julius Caesar. *Caesar's Gallic War*, McDevitte and W. S. Bohn, Translators. (New York: Harper & Brothers, 1869).

The Celtic Sources for the Arthurian Legend, Jon B. Coe and Simon Young (Felinfach: Llanerch Publishers, 1995).

Culhwch and Olwen: An Edition and Study of the Oldest Arthurian Tale, Rachel Bromwich and D. Simon Evans, eds. (Cardiff: University of Wales Press, 1992).

Dafydd ap Gwilym: His Poems, translated by Gwyn Thomas, (Cardiff: University of Wales Press, 2001).

Haycock, Marged, *Legendary Poems from the Book of Taliesin* (Aberystwyth: CMCS Publications, 2007).

The Mabinogi and Other Medieval Welsh Tales, translated by Patrick K. Ford, (Berkeley: University of California Press, 1977).

The Mabinogion, translated by Sioned Davies, (New York: Oxford University Press, 2007).

The Mabinogion, translated by Tales, Charlotte Guest, (London: J.M. Dent and Co, 1906).

The Physicians of Myddfai, translated by John Pughe, (Felinfach: Llanerch Publishers, 1993). Facsimile reprint.

Pliny the Elder. *The Natural History*. John Bostock, Translator. (London: Taylor and Francis, 1855).

Preiddeu Annwn: The Spoils of Annwn, Sarah Higley, trans. (Rochester: University of Rochester The Camelot Project, 2007. Available at http://d.lib.rochester.edu/camelot/text/preiddeu-annwn

"The Tragic Death of Cu Roi mac Dairi", *Ancient Irish* ed. and trans. by Tom P. Cross & Clark Harris Slover (New York: Henry Holt & Co., 1936). Available at http://www.maryjones.us/ctexts/curoi.html

Trioedd Ynys Prydein: The Triads of the Island of Britain, Rachel Bromwich, ed. (Cardiff: University of Wales Press, 2006).

Skene, William F., *The Four Ancient Books of Wales,* (Edinburgh: Edmonston and Douglas, 1868). Available at http://www.sacred-texts.com/neu/celt/fab/fab000.htm

Secondary Sources

Adler, Alfred, "Sovereignty in Chrétien's Yvain", *PMLA,* Vol. 62, No. 2 (Jun., 1947), pp. 281-305.

Arlen, Shelley, *The Cambridge Ritualists: an annotated bibliography of the works by and about Jane Ellen Harrison, Gilbert Murray, Francis M. Cornford, and Arthur Bernard Cook* (Metuchen, New Jersey: Scarecrow Press, 1990).

Armstrong, Edward A., *The Folklore of Birds* (London: Dover Publications, second edn. 1970).

Bhreathnach, Máire, "The Sovereignty Goddess as a Goddess of Death", *Zeitschrift für celtische Philologie,* 39, (1982), pp. 243-260.

Bromwich, Rachel; Jarman, A.O.H; and Roberts, Brynley F., eds., *The Arthur of the Welsh: The Arthurian Legend in Medieval Welsh Literature* (Cardiff: University of Wales Press, 1991).

Bugge, John, "Fertility Myth and Female Sovereignty in 'The Weddynge of Sir Gawen and Dame Ragnell'", *The Chaucer Review,* Vol. 39, No. 2 (2004), pp. 198-218.

Campbell, Joseph, *The Hero With a Thousand Faces* (Princeton: Princeton University Press, 1949).

Cartwright, Jane, *Feminine Sanctity and Spirituality in Medieval Wales* (Cardiff: University of Wales Press, 2008).

Davies, Sioned, *The Four Branches of the Mabinogi* (Llandysul: Gomer Press, 1993).

Eliade, Mircea, *A History of Religious Ideas, Vol. 2: From Gautama Buddha to the Triumph of Christianity,* trans. Willard R. Trask (Chicago: University of Chicago Press,1982).

Ellis, T.P., "Legal references, terms and conceptions in the

Mabinogion", *Y Cymmrodor* 39 (1928), pp. 86 – 148.

Fife, Graeme, *Arthur the King* (New York: Sterling Publishing, 1991).

Frazer, James G., *The Golden Bough* (New York: Collier Books, Macmillan Publishing Company, 1963).

Frazer, James G., *Adonis Attis Osiris: Studies in the History of Oriental Religion* (New Hyde Park, New York: University Books, 1961).

Frazer, James G., "The Sacred Marriage", in *Myths and Motifs in Literature*, David Burrows, ed. (New York: Simon & Schuster, Inc., 1973).

Green, C.M.C., "The Slayer and the King: 'Rex Nemorensis' and the Sanctuary of Diana", *Arion*, Third Series, Vol. 7, No. 3 (Winter, 2000), pp. 24-63.

Green, Miranda, *The Gods of the Celts* (Phoenix Mill, Sutton Publishing Ltd., 2004).

Gruffydd, W.J., *Folklore and Myth in the Mabinogion* (Cardiff: University of Wales Press, 1958).

Gruffydd, W.J., *Math Vab Mathonwy, An Inquiry into the Origins and Development of the Fourth Branch of the Mabinogi, with the Text and a Translation* (Cardiff: University of Wales Press Board, 1928).

Gwyndaf, Robin, *Welsh Folk Tales* (Cardiff: National Museums and Galleries of Wales, 1999).

Herbert, Maire, "Goddess and King: The Sacred Marriage in Early Ireland" in *Women and Sovereignty*, ed. Louise Olga Fradenburg, *Cosmos* 7 (Edinburgh,1992), pp. 264-75.

Jackson, Kenneth, *The International Popular Tale in Early Welsh Tradition* (Cardiff: University of Wales Press, 1961).

Jones, Mary, "Echtra mac nEchach", *Leabhar Buidhe Lecain, Celtic Literature Collective* [Online]. Available at http://www.maryjones.us/ctexts/eochaid.html

Jones, Mary, "Trystan and Esyllt", *Celtic Literature Collective* [Online]. Available at http://www.maryjones.us/ctexts/

trystan.html

Jones, Thomas Gwynn. *Welsh Folklore and Folk-Custom* (London: Methuen & Co. LTD, 1930).

Keefer, Sarah Larratt, "The Lost Tale of Dylan in the Fourth Branch of The Mabinogi", *Studia Celtica*; Jan 1, 1989; 24, ProQuest pg. 26.

Koch, John T., ed., *Celtic Culture: A Historical Encyclopedia* (Santa Barbara: ABC-CLIO, 2006).

Koch, John T., *The Celtic Heroic Age* (Andover: Celtic Studies Publications, 2000).

Kondratiev, Alexi, "Lugus: The Many-Gifted Lord", *An Tríbhís Mhór: The IMBAS Journal of Celtic Reconstructionism* #1, Lúnasa 1997. Available at http://www.imbas.org/articles/lugus.html

Lawrence, Elizabeth A., *Hunting the Wren: Transformation of Bird to Symbol* (Knoxville: University of Tennessee Press, 1997).

Lawton, Jocelyne, *Flowers and Fables: A Welsh Herbal* (Bridgend: Seren Books, 2006).

Lindahl, Carl; McNamara, John; and Lindow, John, eds. *Medieval Folklore* (Oxford: Oxford University Press, 2002).

Loomis, Roger Sherman, *Celtic Myth in Arthurian Romance* (Chicago: Chicago Review Press, 2005).

Mac Cana, Proinsias, *Celtic Mythology* (London: Hamlyn Publishing Group, 1970).

Morrison, Sophia, *Manx Fairy Tales* (London: David Nutt, 1911). Available at http://www.isle-of-man.com/manxnotebook/fulltext/sm1911/p123.htm <Accessed 10 September, 2014>.

Nitze, William A., "The Sister's Son and the Conte del Graal", *Modern Philology*, Vol. 9, No. 3 (Jan., 1912), pp. 291-322.

Owen, Trefor M., *Welsh Folk Customs* (Llandysul: Gomer Press, 1985).

Owen, Morfydd and Jenkins, Dafydd, *The Welsh Law of Women* (Cardiff: University of Wales Press, 1980).

Parker, Will, *The Four Branches of the Mabinogi* (California: Bardic Press, 2005).

Peate, Iorwerth C., "The Wren in Welsh Folklore", *Man*, Vol. 36 (Jan 1936), pp. 1 – 3.

Lord Raglan, "The Hero of Tradition", *Folklore*, Vol. 45, No. 3 (Sep., 1934), pp. 212-231.

Rees, Alwyn, "The Divine Hero in Celtic Hagiology", *Folklore*, Vol. 47, No. 1 (Mar., 1936), pp. 30-41.

Rees, Alwyn and Rees Brinley, *Celtic Heritage: Ancient Tradition in Ireland and Wales* (London: Thames and Hudson, Ltd., 1961).

Rhys, John, *Celtic Folklore: Welsh and Manx* (Oxford: Oxford University Press, 1901).

Roberts, Brynley "*Culhwch ac Olwen*, the Triads, Saints' Lives" in R. Bromwich, A.O.H.

Ross, Anne, *Folklore of Wales* (Stroud: Tempus Publishing Ltd., 2001).

Ross, Anne, *Pagan Celtic Britain: Studies in Iconography and Tradition* (Chicago: Academy Chicago Publishers, 1996).

Schrijver, Peter, *Studies in British Celtic Historical Phonology* (Leiden: Brill Rodopi, 1995).

Sheehan, Sarah, "Matrilineal Subjects: Ambiguity, Bodies, and Metamorphosis in the Fourth Branch of the Mabinogi", *Signs*, 34 (2):(2009), pp. 319-342.

Sikes, Wirt, *Welsh Folklore, Fairy Mythology, Legends and Traditions* (London: Sampson Low, Marston, Searle & Rivington, 1880).

Telyndru, Jhenah, *The Mythic Moons of Avalon* (Woodbury, Minnesota: Llewellyn Publications, 2019).

Telyndru, Jhenah, *Pagan Portals - Rhiannon: Divine Queen of the Celtic Britons* (Winchester, UK: Moon Books, 2018).

Thompson, Stith. *Motif-index of folk-literature: a classification of narrative elements in folktales, ballads, myths, fables, medieval romances, exempla, fabliaux, jest-books, and local legends.* (Bloomington: Indiana University Press,1955-1958). Available at http://www.ruthenia.ru/folklore/thompson/

Trevelyan, Marie, *Folk-Lore and Folk-Stories of Wales* (London: Elliot Stock, 1909).

Valente, Roberta Louise, "Gwydion and Arianrhod: Crossing the Boarders of Gender in Math", *Bulletin of the Board of Celtic Studies* 35 (1988).

Valente, Roberta Louise, "Merched Y Mabinogi: Women and the Thematic Structure of the Four Branches", (Unpublished Ph.D. Thesis, Cornell University, 1986).

Wentersdorf, Karl, "The Folkloric Symbolism of the Wren", *The Journal of American Folklore*, Vol. 90, No. 358 (Apr-Jun 1977), pp. 192 – 198.

Winward, Fiona, "The Women in the Four Branches", *Cambrian Medieval Studies* 34 (1997), pp. 77 – 106.

Wood, Juliette. The Celts: Life, Myth, and Art (Thorsons Publishers, 2002).

Zeiser, Sarah E., "Performing a Literary Paternity Test: "Bonedd yr Arwyr" and the Fourth Branch of *The Mabinogi*", *Proceedings of the Harvard Celtic Colloquium*, Vol. 28 (2008), pp. 200-215.

**MOON
BOOKS**

PAGANISM & SHAMANISM

What is Paganism? A religion, a spirituality, an alternative belief system, nature worship? You can find support for all these definitions (and many more) in dictionaries, encyclopaedias, and text books of religion, but subscribe to any one and the truth will evade you. Above all Paganism is a creative pursuit, an encounter with reality, an exploration of meaning and an expression of the soul. Druids, Heathens, Wiccans and others, all contribute their insights and literary riches to the Pagan tradition. Moon Books invites you to begin or to deepen your own encounter, right here, right now.

If you have enjoyed this book, why not tell other readers by posting a review on your preferred book site.

Recent bestsellers from Moon Books are:

Journey to the Dark Goddess
How to Return to Your Soul
Jane Meredith
Discover the powerful secrets of the Dark Goddess and
transform your depression, grief and pain into healing
and integration.
Paperback: 978-1-84694-677-6 ebook: 978-1-78099-223-5

Shamanic Reiki
Expanded Ways of Working with Universal Life Force Energy
Llyn Roberts, Robert Levy
Shamanism and Reiki are each powerful ways of healing; together,
their power multiplies. *Shamanic Reiki* introduces techniques to
help healers and Reiki practitioners tap ancient healing wisdom.
Paperback: 978-1-84694-037-8 ebook: 978-1-84694-650-9

Pagan Portals – The Awen Alone
Walking the Path of the Solitary Druid
Joanna van der Hoeven
An introductory guide for the solitary Druid, *The Awen Alone* will
accompany you as you explore, and seek out your own place
within the natural world.
Paperback: 978-1-78279-547-6 ebook: 978-1-78279-546-9

A Kitchen Witch's World of Magical Herbs & Plants
Rachel Patterson
A journey into the magical world of herbs and plants, filled with
magical uses, folklore, history and practical magic. By popular
writer, blogger and kitchen witch, Tansy Firedragon.
Paperback: 978-1-78279-621-3 ebook: 978-1-78279-620-6

Medicine for the Soul
The Complete Book of Shamanic Healing
Ross Heaven
All you will ever need to know about shamanic healing and how to
become your own shaman...
Paperback: 978-1-78099-419-2 ebook: 978-1-78099-420-8

Shaman Pathways – The Druid Shaman
Exploring the Celtic Otherworld
Danu Forest
A practical guide to Celtic shamanism with exercises and
techniques as well as traditional lore for exploring the Celtic
Otherworld.
Paperback: 978-1-78099-615-8 ebook: 978-1-78099-616-5

Traditional Witchcraft for the Woods and Forests
A Witch's Guide to the Woodland with Guided Meditations and
Pathworking
Mélusine Draco
A Witch's guide to walking alone in the woods, with guided
meditations and pathworking.
Paperback: 978-1-84694-803-9 ebook: 978-1-84694-804-6

Naming the Goddess
Trevor Greenfield
Naming the Goddess is written by over eighty adherents and
scholars of Goddess and Goddess Spirituality.
Paperback: 978-1-78279-476-9 ebook: 978-1-78279-475-2

Shapeshifting into Higher Consciousness
Heal and Transform Yourself and Our World with Ancient
Shamanic and Modern Methods
Llyn Roberts
Ancient and modern methods that you can use every day to
transform yourself and make a positive difference in the world.
Paperback: 978-1-84694-843-5 ebook: 978-1-84694-844-2

Readers of ebooks can buy or view any of these bestsellers by
clicking on the live link in the title. Most titles are published in
paperback and as an ebook. Paperbacks are available in traditional
bookshops. Both print and ebook formats are available online.

Find more titles and sign up to our readers' newsletter at
http://www.johnhuntpublishing.com/paganism
Follow us on Facebook at https://www.facebook.com/MoonBooks
and Twitter at https://twitter.com/MoonBooksJHP